This book

Laughter & Tears

Has been presented

To *[signature]*

By *[signature]*

The Author.

Dated this day: 14 / 9 2005

First addition Serial Number: 000005

LAUGHTER AND TEARS

Fifty-Four Unique True Stories

D.M. Johnson

MINERVA PRESS
ATLANTA LONDON SYDNEY

LAUGHTER AND TEARS:
Fifty-Four Unique True Stories
Copyright © D.M. Johnson 1999

ISBN 0 75410 715 9

First Published 1999 by
MINERVA PRESS
315–317 Regent Street
London W1R 7YB

Printed in Great Britain for Minerva Press

LAUGHTER AND TEARS

Fifty-Four Unique True Stories

Contents

Introduction

The stories within this book have been mainly written for my grandchildren; I now live in hope that my grandchildren will pass on this book to their own grandchildren in years to come. My own parents' stories of long ago have sadly died with them, and have now been lost for ever. I can now only think of the great loss of those wonderful stories that my parents had told over the years, stories that would have made very good reading by today's standards; I used to sit and listen to my mother's stories with open mouth when I was just a wee boy, just as my own children do today. Because of this, I can not allow my own stories to die with me.

I was born in Berkshire in 1942, just as the war was nearing its end. In those days it was very hard for parents to bring up their children; food was in short supply. Clothing was hand-me-downs. Like many others, I was brought up rough and ready with a secondary education. I am five feet four in height, with fair hair and blue eyes. Before I was born, my seven months pregnant mother was bombed and buried beneath the rubble of her home; neighbours clawed at the rubble with their bare hands to save us both. One month after I was born, the bombing started up again, and I was blown clean out of my mother's arms from the force of the bomb. The bomb had exploded just as my mother and I were passing by a house. When I was found by other nearby people who were searching the rubble for survivors, I was found to be completely covered in soot from head to foot;

only my eyes could be seen from beneath the coat of black dust that had adorned my person.

Some of the short stories within this book may be questionable as to their truth, and may seem to be rather far-fetched, especially by the sceptics. Upon writing this book, I decided that only the truth would enter into it. There are those who may only take a few of these stories to be true, and the remainder to be fiction; but at the end of the day, it doesn't really matter who believes what; for I, and many others who were involved in these stories know it all to be true.

Every person has a story to tell. Placing it down on paper is one thing, having a bad education to apply it is another. I wrote down these true stories mostly as they have happened over the years, and have found that it is far from easy for the likes of myself to put pen to paper.

One of the true stories within this book is about a UFO; I was advised by my own cousin to get this story about a UFO published before it was too late. What he was implying was that in years to come, everyone will be seeing UFOs as an everyday occurrence. Over the recent years more and more true sightings have been seen over a wide area. If all the people that had reported seeing UFOs in the past were speaking in absolute truthfulness, then other people such as myself, who has truly seen a UFO, would then come forward without the fear that he or she would be ridiculed by the media. Because there are lots of false reported sightings by the liars and the meddlers in regard to the sightings of UFOs, there are many such as myself that would not step forward to report a true sighting. There are people out there like myself, who are told by others what they have really seen; I find it to be very strange for those others to say what we have seen, when they themselves were not actually there at the time. The liars, meddlers and sceptics bend the truth to suit themselves financially, or just to get themselves into the eye of the public, in order to make themselves known to be a somebody, rather than a nobody. Like my cousin, I now believe that the whole world will soon see UFOs for themselves, and possibly their occupiers, like my own family have within this lifetime.

It had been widely reported in the media that a huge meteorite was on a collision course with the earth. The scientists say that it's travelling at thirty-two miles per second. If the meteorite was to hit the earth, it would be like rolling a large ball bearing up against a marble. The film *Asteroid*, does not come close to the real disastrous aftermath. One scientist stated that the meteorite would not hit in our lifetime; then it was said by another scientist that it would, within the next eighty years or so. At a later date, it was said by the media that some of the Government scientists had gotten their sums wrong, and it would miss the earth by many miles. Looking at this logically, and with an open mind, how do they know that a meteorite was on a collision course with Earth, from such a far distance in space, and travelling at thirty-two miles per second? One has only to think about that; thirty-two miles per second; that means, as soon as one would have said the word 'second', the meteorite would have then travelled, say, from Salisbury to Fareham. That's some speed. Because of that great speed, the meteorite must be very, very far away. Thinking logically, because of the great distance that this meteorite has to arrive from, I believe that they have information from UFOs to know of such a thing, or that they have something far into deep space that other scientists are totally unaware of. The giant telescopes that they have today could no way see that far into deep space. I personally believe that the information we have upon this meteorite that is heading straight for earth at thirty-two miles per second has come from an outer-space intelligence; I also have a very strong suspicion about where computers first came from.

Other stories within this book are not supposed to be funny, but looking back, they are very funny.

If one was to take into account before reading each story that all the stories that are written within this book are true, then the story that one is reading becomes very much in itself alive. Most true stories that are written can materialise from just one hour or less upon an event within your own life. Some people may think that one must be ten thousand years old, to be able to write fifty true stories or more about themselves; but that is not so. Many such incidents can amount to a hundred stories or more. Every person has a story to tell; so remember, to get the best out of these stories that I have written, one must, upon reading, believe it all, to be true.

The Ghost Dog

At the tender age of seven, I was given a three-month-old puppy-dog by my dear old dad. This puppy-dog was as white as snow. One week after my dear old dad had given me this wonderful-looking puppy-dog, I decided to take him for a walk to a nearby shop. One evening just as the light of day was about to be overcome by darkness, I had entered a shop with my loveable companion. On leaving the shop, my puppy stepped into the gutter as he sniffed the pavement. Whilst my puppy was sniffing the gutter, a car hit him head on.

The driver said, 'Sorry, lad, the dog should not have been on the road.'

I looked at my puppy as he lay on his side in the gutter. There was no movement. As he lay there with his tongue hanging out on one side of his mouth, a small trickle of blood slowly dripped from the corner of his mouth on to the kerb. I then looked up and down the road. There were no other cars in sight. The car that hit my puppy had no reason to have driven along the kerb.

I looked up at the driver and said, 'You killed my dog.'

The driver replied, 'I said sorry, lad. The dog should not have been on the road.'

Again, I said tearfully, 'You killed my dog.' Picking my puppy out of the gutter, I looked at the driver again and said, 'You killed my dog.'

I looked tearfully at my puppy-dog as he lay motionless across both my arms with his head hanging down towards the pavement below. When I returned home, my dear old dad asked me what had happened. After telling him about the unnecessary accident, I added, 'He killed my dog.'

My dad looked at the dead puppy-dog in my arms and said, 'Take him into the back garden and bury him.'

Stepping out into the back garden of my home, on what was now a very dark evening, I dug a deep hole. After digging the hole, I placed the lifeless puppy-dog into its final resting place with a tear. Covering the puppy-dog with a piece of cloth, I pushed, with tears streaming down both cheeks, pushed the soil back into the hole to complete the burial. After the tearful burial, I placed a makeshift cross upon the grave.

That night I could not sleep, with the thoughts of my beloved puppy-dog fixed firmly in mind. The next morning, I got up and went into the back garden to see the grave. Upon opening the back door of the house to enter the garden, I looked down. I thought I was looking at a ghost. Looking up at me with a wagging tail was my puppy-dog. In disbelief, I looked at the white, dirt-soiled puppy-dog for a moment longer, then, with a tear rolling down one side of my cheek, I picked him up. He licked my face all over whilst vigorously wagging his tail. Upon my cuddling him with lots of love and affection, he licked the tears away from my eyes in a playful, loving, boisterous way.

Epilogue

What had happened was that the car did not actually kill the puppy-dog, but had, in fact, only knocked him out. To add to his dilemma, the dog was then buried alive. How he got out of the grave, I will never know. However, I was a happy child.

The Three-Legged Dog

Some years ago I decided to cross-breed a Jack Russell with a Poodle. Both the Poodle and the Jack Russell at the time of the mating were white in colour. The reason I crossed those particular two together was simply because the poodle's fur was made of wool, and the Jack Russell's fur was like pine needles off a Christmas tree. Quite often the pine-needle type fur that had continuously fallen from the Jack Russell would stick to clothing and arm chairs and so on. Being fed up with the everlasting fall-out that was attaching itself everywhere and to everything, I decided to mate my Jack Russell with my next-door neighbour's poodle. Having the full co-operation and permission of my neighbour to experiment with cross-breeding the two dogs, I continued to mate them both. I had the thought clear in mind, that if I mated the two, the offspring should, in theory, be born with woollen coats. To make sure that the mating was successful, I held the Jack Russell bitch tightly within my hands to the floor, whilst the poodle did his dirty work.

The outcome of that event, weeks later, was exactly what was planned. Born between the Jack Russell bitch and the male poodle was a single white fluffy woollen Jack Russell bitch. After the pup was old enough to look after herself, I gave the mother away to my next-door neighbour. I had now seen the end of those annoying loose hairs about the home.

Two years later, the woolly Jack Russell ran out from

the front door of my home, into the path of an oncoming car; in that accident, the woolly Jack Russell lost a front leg; other than this, she was all right.

As time passed, the woolly Jack Russell had become very strong and muscular upon her one front leg. The speed with which she was able to move on three legs was second to none. The woolly Jack Russell had become, as time passed, my wife's dog. For reasons unknown to myself, this woolly Jack Russell had turned very aggressive towards myself. If I were to sit myself down beside my wife upon the sofa; I had firstly to look to see just where the Jack Russell was situated; if I had not done so, then a part of my anatomy would without a doubt be bitten by needle-sharp, snarling, snapping teeth. Sometimes, the Jack Russell would be sitting upon my wife's lap; at other times, when it suited the white ball of fluff, she would hide quietly behind the sofa against the wall. She was a very sneaky, crafty dog. I was, at that time, working nights for a local bus company.

One summer's morning, at approximately eleven o'clock, on getting out of bed, I had run down the stairs with nothing on. Once down the stairs, I then entered the living-room; on entering the living-room, I could see my wife sitting upon the sofa watching the television. Having been filled with high spirits and the touch of the devil, and seeing no sign of the Jack Russell, I pounced upon my wife in all my nakedness; as I did so, the cunning three-legged devil dog appeared from behind the small of my wife's back. On seeing the dog appearing from nowhere, there was no time to move back from the oncoming, snarling, snapping, needle-sharp teeth. The three-legged dog had connected its snapping teeth to a tender part of my naked anatomy. I was now in very great pain. There I was, standing there, with this three-legged dog's jaws shut tight upon the end of my manhood. I wasn't a happy person. The angry little dog was now swinging to and fro with a grip like a vice upon my precious baby-making machine, whilst my wife fell about laughing. The pain was now immense. I stood there with this dog swinging to and fro with tears in my eyes; tears that were not of laughter. I shouted to my wife, '*Get this f—ing thing off me!*' The sight of this dog that was in no way going to let go whilst swinging to and fro with my own body movements had put my wife helpless upon the floor with hysterical laughter. I had to do something fast; *but what*? To make the crazy ball of white fluff let go of my prized manhood, I was able to push both my index fingers into each side of the dog's cheekbone, to force open its lethal needle-sharp snapping teeth, which still held fast upon the end of my baby-making machine. Upon forcing my index fingers further into both sides of the three-legged dog's jaw, I felt almost instant relief, as I succeeded in prizing open the jaws of this three-legged meat eater. The white ball of fluff, upon releasing its firm grip on my baby-making machine, dropped to the floor, then scurried back down behind the settee out of reach and out of sight from any reprisals.

After seeing the three-legged dog disappearing out of sight, I looked back down at my poor bruised baby-making machine, which appeared to be dead as it hung over my hand. My wife's eyes were flooding with tears of laughter, whilst my own eyes were flooded with tears of pain!

The Lost Dog

A few years ago I was driving for a rubbish skip disposal company in Southampton. The name of the company was Tidy's Containers, from Hamble near Southampton. To date, they have ceased trading. To my knowledge, this company was the only rubbish skip disposal company in operation throughout the whole of England at that time. I also believe that they were the very first to introduce the rubbish disposal containers system.

At a later date, this company sold out to another company to make good its full potential for the future. This change-over of ownership had also given its drivers a better deal towards a fair wage at the end of each week. When I myself was driving for Tidy's Containers, I had sometimes to take an empty skip lorry back up to Bristol to another part of that company's premises. In Bristol, I had to collect and bring back to Hamble, a brand-new empty rubbish container from where they were actually being made to order. The payment for doing this was not worth the trip. Throughout the working week, I was picking up full rubbish skips in and around the Southampton area. The drivers in those days were only paid for each single rubbish skip that was to be emptied; this included the emptied skip, returned to the same site of collection. At the end of the week, the amount of skips that one had emptied and returned was totalled to make some sort of a wage. An hourly rate was non-existent. The fewer rubbish skips that one had emptied during the day, the less the wage at the end of the week. Each single skip did not amount to much in terms of money, so one had to keep moving in order to make it pay. The local Millbrook Council rubbish tip, situated in the dock road of Southampton, was the only tip for miles around. Wherever there was a skip to be emptied on pick-up, the journey to the tip and back was quite long. As a rubbish disposal skip lorry driver, one had to race flat-out to collect a full skip-load of rubbish at an appointment site, then one had to drive from the collection site, again flat-out, to the Millbrook tip. It was the same on the return trip. Having done that, one would then race flat-out to the next assignment. It was a tough way to live. If one was well in with the bosses, then one would get all the nearest rubbish skips to the company's home base and the local tip. One would then not need to drive flat-out to make a good weekly wage. The boss's creepers and the snivellers would empty thirty or forty rubbish skips to your weekly total of approximately nineteen. The rubbish skips that I had to empty daily and return, were dotted mostly upon the outskirts of Southampton. There were not enough hours in one day to make good a decent wage in respect of the miles that I had to travel and to endure between each separate trip upon collection and return. The days were long with no incentives.

Whilst driving for that company, I used to take along with myself as a companion on every trip, an Alsatian dog. This Alsatian dog had made himself at home sitting within the cab upon the passenger seat. The name of this Alsatian was quite simply 'Dog'. Dog would not answer to any other name. Some thought this quite funny. Dog would sit upon the passenger seat with the window wide open at all times. If Dog wanted me to stop driving so he could relieve himself, he would look at me and bark. Having to answer his needs, I would then stop the vehicle to comply with his requirements. Though Dog sat near to an open window, he would never jump out; so I thought.

Driving a skip lorry at high speeds along a country road, one would always meet a small country railway humpback bridge. Having always to drive at top speed to make a decent wage, one would never let a little humpback bridge stand in the way. We were known as hell drivers. Time was of the essence. When one met a small humpback railway bridge, the skip lorry would actually leave the ground upon driving at speed over it. The lorry, upon take-off from the brow of the bridge, would sail on through the air, with all four wheels spinning upon an invisible road. The whole weight of the lorry, returning back to earth upon its descent would hit the road with a bang. The chains within the rear that held the skip in place, would swing and bang loudly against the skip itself, and then again against the mechanical arms that lifted the skip on and off. The noise of the banging chains against the skip and lifting frame could be heard echoing all around; it was very loud indeed. Dog and I always left our seats on the wingless plane's re-entry on to the hard tarmac road below, thus further denting the inside of the cab roof and leaving on it an impression of both our heads, after which we were reseated as the vehicle again made contact with the ground. In those days there were quite a lot of small humpback railway bridges about; more so in Hamble itself.

Upon one very hot and sticky summer's day, when Dog and I were out collecting and emptying the skips, I noticed that the fuel tank was quite near to empty. Deciding to return back to base in Hamble to refuel, I placed my foot hard on the accelerator; having not completed that day's collection and returns, time was really against me. I could not really afford to return to base for fuel; but I had no choice, the day was almost gone. Upon reaching the main country road route through Hamble back to base, I had to drive over one of those small humpback railway bridges;

with my foot hard down upon the accelerator, Dog and I, could see up ahead the humpback bridge looming towards us at great speed. Even though the engines upon all tippers in those days were restricted to forty miles per hour, it was still really too fast for what I was now about to do. On reaching the small humpback railway bridge, Dog and I had once again left the road in our wingless aircraft. Suddenly, whilst the lorry was still in mid-air, and the bridge centred somewhere under us, the unexpected happened; Dog jumped out of the window! After Dog had disappeared out of the window and out of sight whilst we were in flight, the skip lorry had returned back to earth upon all four wheels with a bang. The chains rattled against the empty rubbish container and its support arms with an ear-bashing noise.

As soon as the lorry had landed upon its runway, I pulled the skip lorry to a skidding stop five yards further on down the road; on getting out of the cab, slamming shut the door, I raced back on foot to the centre of the bridge, holding the top of my sore head with one hand. Looking over the four feet high brick wall upon the bridge, I could see a train moving away from myself very slowly along the rail tracks, from beneath the bridge that I was now standing upon. The train was almost at a crawling speed. The train had on tow an endless amount of empty open square coal wagons, which looked more like empty shoe boxes upon wheels without the lid. Approximately midway in all these empty shoe box-type wagons, I could see Dog! Dog was sat looking back up at myself with a sorrowful look about his face, sitting inside a single empty coal wagon. Looking back at him from the bridge, I could plainly see that Dog was none the worse for his ordeal. There was nothing that I could do. Dog was going on a long holiday with a one-way ticket. Saddened at the loss of Dog, all I could do was to watch him as he slowly moved on down the track at crawling speed. I wasn't a happy person. As I stood there watching the rail trucks getting smaller and smaller, I said to myself, 'Goodbye Dog! Wherever you are going, have a nice trip.' The train and Dog had slowly disappeared further down the railway track and then out of sight.

Sadly, I returned to the lorry that was parked haphazardly further along the road with its engine still running. After getting back into the driving seat, I looked to the empty passenger seat beside myself. I then, at a much slower speed, drove the lorry back to base. Upon my return to base, I told the company just where to put their job, and what was left of their lorry.

The Dog

During 1988–1990 my family and I lived in Swansea, South Wales. We lived in Wales for approximately two years. The dog that we had with us at that time was an Alsatian. Being a bitch, she would not leave my side. She was very faithful, loving, and very protective towards me. This Alsatian was very intelligent; she would sit and watch my every move and had travelled almost everywhere with me. This Alsatian bitch was definitely a one-man dog.

Upon one icy, bitter-cold day, half-way through the winter months, I was working within my very large shed that was situated at the bottom of the garden. In the shed, I had pre-cut and stockpiled a load of old floor boards into eight-inch lengths to make ready for chopping into kindling. Later that day, as I was chopping the pre-cut wood into kindling, I could see the Alsatian bitch laid upon the shed floor watching my every move as usual. After chopping up a large amount of the kindling upon the chopping block, I would then pick up the loose sticks that were strewn about my feet with both hands; on doing so, I would then walk over to a sack that was situated approximately one yard from the chopping block. Once I had placed the loose kindling into the sack, I then turned to walk back to the chopping block for another handful until there was no more left.

The dog, who was sitting quietly nearby, would watch my repeated actions over and over again, until I had cleared the chopping block of all the loose kindling sticks. After clearing the chopping block of all the loose kindling, I would then re-chop more of the same eight-inch pre-cut wood, into kindling. Chopping up the kindling and then placing it into sacks in large amounts made life a little easier throughout the winter months. Looking at the dog, that was at all times watching whilst laid upon the shed floor, reminded me of someone watching a tennis match; her head would move to and fro, her eyes fixed upon myself walking back and forth from the sack to the chopping block.

Unexpectedly, on that same cold winter's day, whilst I was chopping the wood into sticks of kindling, my faithful companion stood up, then walked towards me at the chopping block. At the chopping block, she sat and watched as I finished the last new batch of kindling. Surprisingly, the dog casually stood up and picked up a few sticks within her jaws, then walked slowly from the chopping block to the nearby sack of kindling. Placing the kindling gently into the top of the open sack, she then turned to look at me and wagged her tail in a very cocky and showy manner. I was totally gobsmacked and amazed by what she had just done. I was a happy person. After the dog had done this surprisingly unexpected good deed, she then walked back to her watching position upon the floor. I was so over the moon by what she had just done, I tried to get her to do it again, but she would not! Not even with several further attempts at encouragement. I was very disappointed.

That day was a very special day to me, as stupid as it may sound; I always treasure that moment. Six months later, this wonderful dog was killed by a car.

The Rat

In 1990 I lived in Swansea, South Wales. The story that I am about to tell you now is, in my view, a story of obedience, determination, fulfilment, intelligence, loyalty and friendship. Those six magic words were naturally embodied in a very close friend of mine. Of course, with those ingredients, it must be obvious to you that I am talking about a dog. This dog wasn't just any old dog; in fact it was an Alsatian. This Alsatian bitch was almost human; it was a dog that would, on most occasions, carry out commands to dropping point; even if it meant her own death in the execution of her duties. She was the type of dog that could only exist in people's dreams, a dog that every dog-owner would love to have for themselves. This Alsatian bitch was almost half the size again of a full grown Alsatian male dog. It's quite normal in most breeds, for the male dog to be almost twice the size of the bitch; but this dog had it all, she was unusually enormous in size, very pretty, obedient, and protective. This story encapsulates just one of the wondrous events that I for one will never forget.

Upon one cold day in the winter months of 1990, this wondrous dog had tried to help me to catch a very big rat at the bottom of the garden in Wales. At the bottom of my garden, I had a very big wooden shed that was twenty feet long, eight feet wide, and eight feet high. Not too far away from this big shed, was a very large kennel. The kennel was obviously for the Alsatian to sleep in at nights to guard whatever there was to guard within the large shed. This dog had two different types of barks; one of the dog's barks was for when there was an unauthorised person about the property; the other was when there was something wrong, or she wanted to show me something. Both barks were clearly distinctive. The rat that the dog and I tried to catch had run under a stack of long timber, that was situated just past the big shed at the bottom of the garden; on seeing the rat at the same time as myself, the dog and I gave chase. As I chased the rat into one end of the timber stack, the dog simultaneously ran to the other end of the timber stack. We both searched in and around the timber stack for the rat without success; after half an hour had passed, we had both given up all hopes on catching the rat. Night time was now upon us, it was time to call it a day. Later that same evening, I just gotten out of the bath as the dog had started to call me. My wife then walked into the bathroom and said, 'The dog wants you?'

I replied, 'The dog has plenty of food and water, so it cannot be that she's out of food, she will have to wait until the morning, it's now pouring down with rain!'

The next morning, I walked on down to the end of the garden to where the dog was situated. At the bottom of this garden was a partition fence that had divided the garden into two, and both the shed and the dog's kennel were situated on the other side of the partition. On reaching the fence, I leaned over to look into the kennel, to see just where the dog had disappeared to. The dog was nowhere to be seen. Looking in the direction of the big shed that was to the left, I could see that the door to the shed was open. To look into the shed from my present position was not easy. As it had no windows, the shed was lacking daylight; I could barely see into the shed as I strained my eyes from my leaning position upon the fence. Upon my eyes becoming accustomed to the darkened inside of the shed from the outside, I could see the outline of the dog laid down, just inside the entrance. I then left the partition fence to enter the shed. At the entrance, I could barely see her amid the cloak of darkness within. Looking down at her laid upon the floor in the windowless darkened shed, I could see that she was making strange jerking movements with her head and nose, that I had never seen her do before. As she lay there, I thought that she must be ill. I looked at her with concern and asked, 'What's the matter with you girl?'

The dog continued to make the same unnatural jerking movements with her nose as before; I was now quite worried about her. Whilst I was still standing at the shed entrance looking in, I had then suddenly realised that she was trying her hardest to tell me something. I then looked further into the dark shed, to where her nose appeared to be jerking and pointing; to my surprise, there upon the floor was this very big rat. It was mangled, very dead and very wet. I was quite sure, on seeing the dead rat, that it was the very same one that we both had tried to catch the day before; it had a distinctive kink in its tail. I then looked back to where the dog was still lying upon all fours; as I did so, the dog half-wagged her tail as my eyes focused upon hers.

The dog then very slowly stood up upon her feet and walked tiredly out of the shed, then back into her kennel. I looked at her, full of joy at her fulfilment upon her accomplishment and determination to catch the rat in my absence. I then picked up the mangled rat and threw it over the hedge of my garden into a field. As I turned to face the dog, I could see that she was now fast asleep and snoring within her kennel. She was absolutely plum-tuckered out. I have never ever known this dog to sleep in the daytime. That wonderful dog had stayed up all night, just to show me the rat.

The Yeti

Upon a farm in the Isle of Wight some years ago, I had a very large chicken-run. Early one morning upon getting out of bed, I found that all the chickens were running around loose, outside their pen. Inspecting the chicken-wire that had made up their enclosure, I found that the wire had been pulled up from the ground. The size of the hole that had been made was enormous; it measured approximately five feet in height and three feet in width. I just knew that it could not have been a fox; whatever made this hole in the mesh wire was very big indeed. After repairing the damage to the mesh wire and then catching all the chickens, I replaced them in the enclosure. After putting them back into the enclosure, I walked around to see my next-door neighbour, the farm's hedge cutter, to ask if he had heard anything in the night; he said that he had not heard a thing. I was none the wiser as to what it could have been.

Whatever it was that entered the enclosure repeated the same destructive move three more nights in a row. On the fourth day, late in the evening, I had returned from the local village pub; it was a very dark winter's night with no moon, and I could hardly see my own hand in front of myself. Upon reaching my home after walking back down from a very dark country lane, I had to enter through a gate, that gave access to the two separate back-to-back tied farm cottages that my neighbour and I occupied. Entering the gate in pitch darkness, I passed the first cottage that ad-joined my own cottage at the rear. I then went through a second gate that gave access to my own front door, and a very large garden that was surrounded by fields. After shutting the gate behind myself, I could see something rather shadowy and frightening near to the chicken-run ahead. Whatever it was, it was standing tall and quite near to where the wire had been pulled up previously. Straining my eyes into the darkness, the silhouette looked something like a giant bear or the mythical yeti. The creature must have stood approximately seven feet high. The night was so dark that the moon could only cast a little light through the cracks of the very dark clouds that had engulfed the whole sky. I normally carried a torch, but upon this night, when I most needed it, I had left it within the cottage. Edging myself nervously forwards towards the shadowy figure, inch by inch, I suddenly stopped in my tracks as the silhouetted figure moved slightly. On standing still, I could see a furry outline to the silhouette. Whatever it was, it was standing upright and looking straight back at me; I felt it watching my every move.

It was very eerie and frightening, and my hands had started to sweat. Taking a deep breath, with small steps, I moved approximately six inches further towards it, then stopped. Upon stopping, I could hear slow heavy breathing coming from the direction of the ghostly figure before me. If my calculations were right, I was now approximately five yards away from this hairy giant, which had not moved from its present position. A small amount of light was now showing through the cracks of the darkened clouds as I stood there. This small amount of light gave me a slightly better view of a very dark head with pointed ears. As I was about to move again, the unidentified shape swayed slightly, thus making my heart beat quite fast; I was going to go no further. I was about to backtrack to get myself a torch from the cottage, when the moon suddenly broke through the dark clouds that had blotted out the light of the sky. The bright moonlight made the shadowy creature clear to me. I felt a large sense of relief run through the whole of my body as I could now see standing there a very large husky dog. The husky dog was standing up upon his rear legs, with the front legs stretched high above his own head, upon the inside enclosure wire, looking back in my direction. As I stepped towards him, the dog wagged his tail. He was very quiet and friendly.

After making a fuss of this rather large dog, I pulled him on back through the hole that he had once again made on entry into the chicken-run. Taking the dog by the collar, I led it back through the two gates to the outside road; I then crossed the road to a cottage on the other side. On arrival at the front door, I knocked to see if there was anyone at home. A man opened the door. I asked the man if the dog belonged to him, and he replied, 'Yes! I wondered where he had gone to.'

I then told the owner what his dog had been doing for the past few days. I also told him, 'Because of my frightening experience, if I see the dog over in my chicken-run again, I will shoot it.'

The owner of the big bear-like dog said nothing in reply. Taking the dog by the collar, he then turned to go back into the cottage. I did however, at a later date, become quite friendly with the dog-owner.

Winning the Football

In the old days to be able to do the football coupons, one would have to be twenty-one years old.

The very first football coupon that I filled in was when I was living upon a farm in the Isle of Wight. Upon the back of the coupon, it was, then, any three draws and four aways; the front of the coupon was eight draws for twenty-four points as it is today. What I played that week upon the coupon was the three draws. That following week, I found that I had the three draws up. I was a happy person. How much money had I won, I hadn't a clue. The jackpot for twenty-four points in those days was one million pounds. After checking the results, I left my home to go across the road to see a friend. My friend answered the door to my knock, and with a husky dog standing close to his heels said, 'Yes!'

I then told him of my three draws, and asked how much money did he think that I might have won.

This friend of mine said in excitement, 'Blimey mate! You could have won thousands.'

I then, trying not to show my excitement, coolly replied, 'Is that right!'

'Yes! Thousands,' he repeated hysterically, in happiness for myself.

I thanked him for his help, then walked casually, and as if very coolly, away from his home. Upon walking across the road and entering my own little farm cottage, I picked up the coal scuttle, full to the top with coal dust, then threw it high into the air, shouting, 'Yeah!' at the very top of my voice. The coal dust made rather a mess over a wide area on the living-room carpet.

The next day, I received my winnings through the post. Upon tearing open the envelope with excitement, I took out the enclosed cheque. After looking at the cheque, I came back to reality with a thud, as my eye fell upon the amount. I had won one and sixpence (eight and a half pence in today's coinage). I then looked around the room at the black coal dust that had fallen across the carpet; it was a mess. Removing the coal dust from the living-room carpet took my wife and I several days. In those days, a Hoover was non-existent for the ordinary peasant like myself.

My wife wasn't a happy person.

The Fly

On 28th July, 1997 I had overslept into the late hours of the morning. Whilst I was asleep, there was a fly zooming around the room. I could hear the buzzing of the wings penetrating the air as it flew about the room in my sleep. Determined not to let the noise of the buzzing fly disturb my slumber further, I continued to drift in and out of sleep.

The fly awoke me by walking about my face. After scratching, and waving my hand about my own face to drive away the annoying fly, I turned over upon my right side to continue my blissful sleep. The fly had no intention of letting me sleep on. Once again the annoying fly buzzed around the room and then landed back upon my face, whilst I was just slipping into a deep sleep. Smacking my own face hard with the flat of my own hand with a disturbed grunt, I missed the fly. The hard smack to my own face almost awakened me fully; upon my throwing several curses at the fly, it continued to buzz about the room. In my annoyance I turned over to sleep upon my left side, but as I had did so, the fly once again landed upon the side of my face. Without moving a single part of my body, I lay there in silence with my head upon the pillow and with my eyes now wide open. The fly was also now not moving. The fly was now motionless upon its landing site; it was now a waiting game between the two of us to see who was going to move first.

After about a minute or so, the fly started to skate about my face. Smacking the side of my own face once again with the flat of my hand, I had again missed the annoying fly. I finally succumbed to defeat, and was forced to get up.

Ten minutes later, whilst having a late breakfast, this being a bowl of cornflakes, the fly reappeared in the kitchen to further annoy me. Picking up a rolled-up newspaper, I proceeded to smack the fly into oblivion to end my torment. Succeeding in a well-aimed blow upon the fly, bringing the newspaper down upon it whilst it was still in flight, the end of the newspaper and the blood-splattered squashed fly entered my own cereal bowl, thus, knocking the cereal bowl from the table to the floor. My wife, who was also having a bowl of cornflakes, upon seeing the end of the newspaper and the fly entering the milk within my bowl, was sick. On seeing my wife throwing up, I looked down to the floor. Upon doing so, I could see the cat lapping up the spilt milk and the cornflakes with the additional mixed vomit that had flooded the floor near to the leg of the table from my wife. I then was also sick. The more my wife heaved and sickened, the more I sickened. There we both were, sickening and heaving, and all because of the fly.

The Dead Cat

I will always remember an incident that happened upon the road whilst I was driving a tipper lorry. Whilst driving along a road in Southampton, I saw something lying in the road that made me violently sick and very ill. But before I tell you yet another true tale from the past, I must tell you a little bit more about myself. In short, if I feel sick and then vomit, I must shut my eyes; if I did not shut my eyes whilst vomiting, and looked upon the first lot of vomit that I had discharged from the depths of my stomach, I would then violently vomit again. I have yet to meet another person with a weaker stomach then my own.

This story took place upon a very hot day, and in my view, what I had seen that day would make others feel as I did. As I was driving down a very grimy and dusty road in Northam, Southampton, I noticed in the middle of the road a dead cat. The cat was on first appearance intact. There were no visual marks to show that the cat had been knocked over and killed by another vehicle. The road that day was busier then usual; it was full of very heavy vehicles going up and down in both directions. The road was a back road, that led into an avenue of industrial building prem- ises, such as the dust-carts, coal yards, sand and ballast, scrap-yards, building yards and the gasworks etc. The road itself was approximately three miles long. The road and all the very old buildings were engulfed by the coal dust and grime that was emitted from an array of premises, and heavy vehicles that had run the length of the road, all day and every day. The name of this long industrial back road was in two halves. Half the road was named Britannia Road; the other half was named Albert Road. This old industrial road was almost at the waterfront of the river where many cargo boats and barges would unload. The transport activity upon this road was enormous and very noisy. Upon this same long dusty industrial road, I myself had been travelling up and down consecutively for three days, transporting top soil. The top soil had to be delivered to a new building site at the end of Albert Road, from an old building site at the start of Britannia Road. The day was very hot and dry. Sitting within a lorry upon a hot day in those days without a fan cooler of some kind, was at times unbearable. My person was saturated with sweat as I drove along the long dusty road under the blazing sun. Whilst I was upon one of my journeys to deliver a load of top soil from the old building site, I noticed the dead black cat in the middle of the road; midway between Britannia Road and Albert Road. The large cat was very big as cats go, and it looked to have been heavily pregnant. This extra large dead cat that was in the middle of the road, was untouched all day by the heavy passing lorries that ran in both direc-tions. On passing the dead cat towards the late afternoon, I held tight my stomach until I had reached the end of Britannia Road, my destination for reloading. Seeing the dead cat made me feel a little queasy every time I passed it in either direction. On one of my return trips with an empty lorry, I could see that the cat had now been moved by overtaking vehicles into the overtaking lane. The cat was now situated in the path of oncoming traffic that was going in the opposite direction to myself. I was dreading my return trip down that road when loaded. Upon reaching the loading site, I waited my turn to be loaded by a JCB. After reloading top soil into my lorry, I then drove the lorry back off from the site on to the road. Once again, I was travelling the same route back along that busy road to the new building site for the off-loading. I was now almost midway between Britannia Road and Albert Road, where I had last seen the dead cat.

As I was driving along, my eye fell upon what was now a squashed and mutilated dead cat, just ahead of myself; the cat had been popped under the wheels of a passing juggernaut, as if it were a balloon; I felt quite ill upon seeing the state of this cat before me. After seeing the mutilated cat ahead, I had no choice but to pull over to the kerbside and stop the vehicle. As I sat looking out from the driver's side window from between the fingers of the hand that was shielding my eyes from the squashed dead cat, almost opposite where I had pulled in, I could see the cat being squashed several more times, with parts being torn from its body and flipped into the air by the wheels of other passing lorries; one piece of blood-covered flesh hit the driving door upon my lorry with a thud, and held fast to the paintwork below myself. I could hear the sound of squelching, as the cat was again and again run over by other lorries that had passed me by. There was blood and guts everywhere; parts of unborn kittens were mutilated and strewn about the busy road in an unsightly manner, it was a right mess.

After pulling up to the side of the road to allow other vehicles to pass me by, and after looking at the cat from in between my fingers, I hung my head out of the opened cab door window to be violently sick. All the food and drink that I had consumed that day went out of the window. As I vomited on to the road outside, I could see it mixing with blood and bits of guts that now spread close to the wheels of my own stationary lorry. Minute particles of flesh, guts and blood were being thrown up and off the heavy wheels of the other lorries as they trundled on by. I could see the piece of cat's flesh that had moments before stuck to the door below myself, start to slide down off the smooth wet paintwork to the road, as I leaned out of the window to be sick. My eyes filled with tears from the strain of being so violently sick. I wasn't a happy person.

Wiping the tears from my eyes, I looked out to the other side of the busy road to another lorry that was parked opposite myself, but facing the other way. Looking across at the other lorry through sparkling watery eyes, I could see that it was a Southampton dust-cart. The make and model of the dust-cart was a Denies, the type that had sliding shutters upon each side. The dust-cart was a dark green in colour. I thought that the dust-cart had pulled up upon the opposite side of the road to collect the dead cat, but I was wrong. As I wiped away the watery sparkling sick tears from my eyes, I could see that the driver of the parked dust-cart was sat within his cab; on seeing the other driver, I could see that he too was hanging his head out of the cab window being violently sick. Some parts of the squashed and mutilated cat had now moved with the traffic to both sides of the road. Seeing the other driver leaning out of his window and being violently sick, had once again made me throw up. We both must have looked a right sight to other passing motorists, what with him on one side of the road hanging out of the window being sick, and myself upon the opposite side simultaneously doing the same. We could hear each other retching clearly. As I wiped away the tears from my eyes with my left arm, I reached down with my right hand to restart the lorry. I just had to get away from the mess that the other vehicles were spreading about the road. The other driver simultaneously restarted his dust-cart. As we both were about to move off, we both simultaneously looked across to each other's face. I did not know who was the more surprised out of the two of us, as we both looked upon one another on driving off; I just could not believe whom I was now looking at; it was a most unusual coincidence, something that could never be repeated. The other person whom I was now looking across at, as we both had simultaneously started to drive off, was my own brother! The pair of us looked at each other for a moment, then began to fall about laughing within the cabs of our lorries as we had both moved away simultaneously from that place of discomfit. Whilst driving down the road, I could not stop laughing over the occurrence. I still had tears in my eyes as I drove further on down the road. But this time, it was not through being sick, it was from laughter. I then decided to take a different route back to the beginning of Britannia Road once I had off-loaded the top soil, for I did not want to go through all that again.

After I had reached my journey's end, and finally off-loaded, I decided to take a new but longer route back to the beginning of Britannia Road. On driving along the new route, I again burst into fits of laughter as I then saw my brother once again, driving past in the opposite direction. He too, had picked a new route to avoid the cat. As we were both about to pass each other, he held his head out of his cab window to mimic vomiting; we both roared with laughter as we continued on our different ways.

The Bonfire Cat

When I was nineteen I worked on a building site as a tea boy. Every day I had to leave the site to go and order in provisions from the local butcher's shop, in Oak Tree Road, near Woodmill, Southampton. The items that I had to buy were a crate of milk and at least four packets of tea. In days long gone, most of the butchers had within their shops a butcher's cat. These butcher's cats were interbred down through the years. They had grown to an enormous size. People of today cannot really comprehend the enormity of these great cats, but there is still at this present time people out there who know exactly what I'm saying, when I refer to the big butcher's cats of days long gone. These large butcher's cats, would grow to the size of a miniature Collie; believe me, that was big. If an ordinary full-grown house cat was placed alongside one of those big butcher's cat, the full-grown house cat would look more like a kitten standing beside its mother.

These giant cats used to sit about the shop patiently waiting for the butcher to throw down upon the floor the off-cuts of raw meat that had been stripped from the bones after a joint of meat had been cut to order, or cut and prepared for display purposes in the shop windows. Upon the floors of the butcher's shops in those days was sawdust; the sawdust was thrown down to stop the blood and the bits of meat sticking to the wooden floors. These big cats used to sit upon the sawdust on both sides of the counter waiting for a tasty titbit to drop their way. Sometimes, the butcher would throw down to the big cats odd pieces of raw meat that he had just cut from a joint upon the big wooden table. Several times throughout the day, the butcher would clean the table by scrubbing it with soap and water to comply with the hygiene regulations.

Within the very same year of discovering the big cats' existence, the law changed their hygiene regulations, to stop these great cats from entering the inside of the butcher's shops where the many different types of meats were stored or sold. Because of this change in the law, the big cats slowly disappeared over the years, perhaps now totally extinct.

Now that I have enlightened you about those big cats, it is time to take my story that much further forward in regards to my own personal involvement with one of the big cats. This story about the bonfire cat really starts here.

It was on 5th November, 1951, I was nine years old; bonfires were everywhere in those days. Many of the streets in the old days were like *Coronation Street*. Bonfire night in those days was a very big thing to look forward to. Most of the people who lived in the Northam, Southampton area, at the end of the year placed all their burnable rubbish outside by the front doors of their homes; it was then left to all the local kids from each street to carry or drag all burnables to the nearest waste ground. The war had destroyed many homes by turning them into piles of rubble. As time passed, the rubble had been cleared from the bombing sites, and the ground was then laid to waste. Upon each waste ground where houses once stood, one would find a heavy pigs' swill bin. The pigs' swill bins were for all the local people to throw their unwanted food waste into. Nothing was ever wasted, everything had its uses in those days. This waste food from the swill bins was collected each week by a local pig breeder to help him to keep the feeding cost down.

Every year, the bonfires upon those waste grounds were

built very high. It was a challenge to see what street could build the biggest bonfire. Sometimes, after a bonfire had been built or was near to completion, they would get raided at night by other kids from another street. These kids from another street would raid the bonfires from different streets or roads to ensure that their own bonfire was going to be the biggest and the best. If the bonfire was completed before time, guards were situated around the bonfire after school hours until bonfire night. There were times when an all out war would erupt between the kids from the other streets or from other parts of the town. Pirating of burnable materials from the bonfire sites was a serious game. Catapults and home-made bows and arrows were frequently used upon some of the pirate kids, to get back what was stolen; the hospitals in those days were never short of casualties. As time passed, and the bonfires were all built to completion, some parents would take it in turns to stay up all night to protect the bonfires from the raiders until the big night.

Bonfire night was finally upon us. It was now seven o'clock in the evening. Seven o'clock in the evening was the traditional time in those days for the lighting of the bonfires. The bonfires were now all set alight everywhere with the sound of fireworks echoing throughout the dark night air.

The bonfire that I was attending with my pals had now started to get very hot. The sky lit up over a wide area with a colourful red glow as the fireworks were being let off in their hundreds. The crackling of burning wood upon the fire, and the illuminating floating sparks could be seen and heard over a great distance. The dark sky was ablaze with an array of colourful lights from bonfires all over; an aroma of smoke from the fires, and the sulphur from the fireworks filled the air. It was a great night. Hundreds of people were in attendance.

As the evening went on and the fireworks and sparklers were running short, a few of the school kids, as well as myself, started to get very boisterous and fed up. I, and many others kids, were now playing in the light and smoke of the bonfire. Not too far away from the bonfire was a pigs' swill bin; a few of us were running around the bin in a frenzy of excitement to pass the remaining hours. As we played around the pigs' swill bin, I noticed upon the ground near to the swill bin a very large dead cat. The dead cat was the biggest cat that I and my school chums had ever seen; it was a giant of a cat. There wasn't a mark to be seen upon this big cat, so it was impossible to determine the cause of death. A passing parent remarked that it was a butcher's cat, that's why it was so big. Picking up the dead butcher's cat by its very long fat tail, I dragged it nearer to the very hot bonfire. My aim was to throw it into the bonfire, just to see it burn. Holding the big cat by its fat tail with two hands, because it was far too big and heavy for such a small nipper as myself to lift, I started to swing the cat around, and around, and around my person to pick up enough momentum in speed to let fly the cat into the hot fire. As I gained enough speed to let fly the big cat, my plan was interrupted by the unexpected. The big heavy butcher's cat had parted from its fat tail. As I held the departed tail in both hands like a furry snake, I looked up skywards to see where the big cat had gone too. On looking up, I could see the enormous big cat coming straight back down at speed above my head; it was too late for me to move out of the way. This big butcher's cat came back down squarely upon the top of my head. The weight and the impact of the big cat knocked me clear to the ground into a sitting position. As the giant cat made contact with my head, it immediately fell to pieces. It was full of maggots. The maggots absolutely covered my entire head, face, and clothing; I was a mess. All my friends jumped about me to clear away the mass of maggots from off my head and shoulders. I then took off most of my clothing to get rid of all the maggots that had found their way down to the inside of my shirt. I wasn't a happy child. Parents nearby fell about laughing along with all my chums. The big butcher's cat, at that time, was the biggest that I had ever seen as a nipper; the maggots were next in line, they were very fat and squiggly. All my chums started to laugh once again, just as a parent threw the big cat with its giant squiggly maggots, that were still dropping to the ground in abundance, upon the very hot bonfire. That was one cat that I will never forget.

The Cesspit

This story that I am about to tell you goes back to the year 1967. Half-way through the summer months of that year, I was working upon a farm in the Isle of Wight. On this farm there was a very large dry concrete pit that was situated not too far from the milking sheds. Around the perimeter of the dry pit was a four-foot railing. The length of this dry pit was twenty-five yards. The width was ten yards. The depth was two foot with the safety railings being set at two feet higher upon the upper ground level of the pit. Inside this pit was a bedding of hay, a water trough, and a few young calves that were all approximately a little over three feet in height. At one end of this dry pit was another pit, that had dropped down to a deeper depth; this deep pit was an extension to the first one. It measured approximately ten yards in width, but only six yards in length with a depth of five foot. There was no dividing safety rail between the two when standing in the pit.

The smaller deeper pit to one end was used as a cesspit for all the cows' excrement and urine. Both pits were situated upon the farm to act also as a roundabout in the centre of the farm's inner road. If one were to picture a frying pan, with farm buildings running around the outer edge of the pan, with an inner ring road also running parallel to the outer farm buildings within the pan, and then having the pits situated to the centre of the pan, this also will give one an overall picture of the total layout of the farm.

After the cows had been milked within the milking sheds, they were then chased out of the sheds, on to the inner farm road. Once the cows were upon the inner farm road, they were then chased once again past the pits, then further on towards a dirt track road; before the cows could make a mess upon the concrete. The dirt track road, this now being described as the handle upon the frying pan, led back into the fields. After all the cows had been milked the milking sheds and the tarmac road then had to be washed down with a powerful hose. The washing down of the cow sheds and the tarmac road with the hose would then wash all the cows' excrement and urine on down into the drains. The drains ran back into the smaller of the two pits, this then being officially known as a cesspit. All the water and excrement being washed down into the drains and then on out into the small, but deep, cesspit, would very quickly fill the cesspit to the point of overflowing. 'The contents of the cesspit were very loose and soft, and filled the surrounding air with a foul smell; and yet, the overflow from the cesspit did not run into its neighbouring dry pit, for the neighbouring dry pit was situated upon a slightly higher level. Explaining the layout of the dry pit as opposed to the already filled slightly lower cesspit is necessary, in order for one to understand the following story.

My story about what happened within this cesspit really begins here. Upon one summer's day, I was told by the farmer to give the chief herdsman a hand within the dry pit. On entering the dry pit, I asked the chief herdsman what it was that he wanted me to do. He replied by saying; 'Come with me, we have got to clean out the hoofs upon the calves feet.'

Following him now to the other end of the dry pit towards the cesspit end, where the pit dropped on down to a deeper depth, we had come in contact with the calves, which were standing quite near to the edge of the deep open cesspit. The chief herdsman then grabbed hold of one small calf; not knowing much about farming, I watched his every move. Within the chief herdsman's hand was a cattle knife for hooking the stones from out of the cattle's hoofs; this cattle knife was also used for the trimming of the hoofs. Being new to farm work and rather green behind the ears, I asked the chief herdsman how best could I help him. He replied, 'I want you to hold still the calf whilst I clean out the hoofs.' The chief herdsman, who was a very mischievous person, told me to place a leg over the back of the calf, so that the calf could be held tight between my legs. Placing a leg over the calf's back, as opposed to riding a horse; the chief herdsman suddenly shouted, 'No, not that way! You will have to turn around and hold on to the tail.' I then dismounted the calf to turn myself around; I then remounted the calf in order to face into the opposite direction as ordered. Sitting upon this calf the wrong way round was not easy, for both my feet were not quite able to touch the concrete floor. The chief herdsman knelt down upon one leg; on doing so, he lifted the rear foot of the calf to hook out the stones whilst I hung on to its tail to keep my balance; I was now sat looking down upon the chief herdsman, as he scraped upon the hoof of the calf; as the calf tried to move about, I was not totally able to keep my balance. Whilst sitting upon the back of the calf, I held tight on to its tail for dear life. I was trying to hold still the calf from my unbalanced position; on doing so, I looked down to see what he was doing with the knife; if I was going to learn anything, then there's no time like the present. The chief herdsman was knelt down upon one knee and holding one hoof slightly off the ground. I could then see from my unsettled rocking position upon the calf, that he was up to no good. As I continued to watch him, a grin appeared upon one side of his stupid face. He then looked back up at me with an even bigger smile, but it was too late; the chief herdsman had smacked hard the rear of the calf, then shouted and hollered whilst clapping his hands in a frenzied manner; the calf had taken fright, and tried its hardest to buck me off from its back; eventually, after my hanging on for dear life to its tail, the calf succeeded in throwing me from its back, straight into the cesspit; on entering into cesspit with a backward flying dive from the back of the calf, I sank right under and out of sight. I was not a happy person.

Upon resurfacing, I could just see the chief herdsman laughing as he ran along the dry pit to reach the upper roadway. Covered from head to toe in crap, I managed to clamber out from the cesspit; my person was totally engulfed in excrement and urine. Jumping into the nearest horse trough to quickly dilute my suit of excrement and urine, I tried frantically to rid myself of all. I was violently sick upon entering the horse trough. The excrement was in my mouth, up my nose, inside my clothing, it was everywhere; after completely submerging myself within the horse trough, I was then left with a thin layer of the foul-smelling stuff upon my person. Whilst I was heaving and being violently sick, I managed to leave the water trough in the dry pit; pulling myself up and over the safety railings to reach the road, I was able to grab at the fire-hose that was situated upon the farm road. Having the fire-hose now full on, I began to hose myself clean; whilst hosing myself down, I could see the chief herdsman rolling about with laughter beside a barn. I then took off all my clothing and threw them down upon the ground in temper. I must have been under that hose for an hour or more. My stomach felt as if it had been turned inside out from the strain of being continuously sick. As the days and months passed by, I became a much wiser person.

The Stolen Radio

When I was twenty-four years of age, I met a friend who looked as if he were well and truly down in the dumps. He gave the appearance that he was not a happy person. Upon meeting my friend, I asked what was troubling him; he then told me that he had been ripped off by a well-known taxi-driver. This taxi-driver was also well known for tax evasions and being a bit of a hard man, in and around the Southampton area. My friend, who was not a fighting man, had asked me to get back a radio that the taxi-driver had stolen from him under protest in broad daylight. I said to my friend that I will give it a try, but not to expect too much as he might have sold it.

We both knew where the taxi-driver lived, and that he was living alone. It was now late into the evening, and there were no stars or moon to light the way; it was a very dark night. It was almost impossible to see where one was walking. The street lighting in those days, if there was any, was very poor. Having a plan of action that might work, I told my friend to wait down the road and I would see what I could do for him. Upon reaching the taxi-driver's house and walking through the front gate, I knocked on the front door, but there was no answer. I could see the radio that my friend had described to me, through the front window upon the inner ledge that was partially obscured by the heavy inside curtains. After waiting approximately five minutes, I walked past the front door of the house, to turn left at the side entrance towards the rear of the house;

taking the next left, placed myself to the rear of the house. At the rear of the house, there was no one to be seen. Unable to gain access to the rear of the house, I continued to take the next left turn; having now walked almost completely around the building in a horseshoe manner to the opposite side of the house, I could just see the front garden gate further up the path, where I had first made my entrance. At the side of the house, as I walked further along the path, I spotted an open window. The window was a very small window; it had firstly a sheet of frosted glass set within the lower part of the wooden frame, with a small opening window situated above within the same frame. The small wooden window frame, when fully opened, measured approximately one foot square; but from one corner to the other corner, measured thirteen inches. With a very tight squeeze, one could manipulate the body on through this small window with careful calculation of body distortion. I decided there and then that this taxi-driver was not going to get away with it this time; my mission was very clear to me. What little light that had momentarily allowed me to see the garden gate that was further along the path, had now faded into total blackness; I could not now see my own hand as I felt for the open window above myself. Finding the small window by touch, I climbed approximately four feet up the wall to gain access to the small window. So far my mission was going fine.

Entering the window feet first was not so easy, I almost got stuck permanently within the small window frame, even though I had calculated my body distortion with every move. It had taken me an hour trying to get myself through this very small window with great difficulty. I was not about to be beaten. I was now positioned with half my body in and half my body out of the window. I could not see the footpath below the window as I struggled on through. As I blindly moved backwards through the window into the house, with my legs dangling on the inside, I tried to feel with my feet something solid that would take my body weight, apart from the flooring that was somewhere further down beneath myself. Now almost in, apart from my arms and shoulders, I felt something underfoot. As I slowly slid further into the very dark room, by wriggling the remainder of my body on through the tiny window frame, without warning, I fell on through into the unlit room. Upon landing one of my feet had gone straight down into an open toilet pan. On my final entry, I found myself to be sitting upon a hard concrete floor in a most uncomfortable distorted position, in total darkness. In my unorthodox and untimely landing, I almost twisted and broke my leg in the fall. Getting back up off the floor from my present position was not easy. Taking my wet foot out from within the toilet pan as I simultaneously struggled to my feet, I stretched out an arm to feel what was in front of me. I did not have to stretch far in either direction before coming in contact with the inside walls. I could just see a very faint flicker of light illuminating the crack of a door frame as my eyes became slightly accustomed to the dark; fumbling for the handle with both hands, I was able to open the door very slowly and quietly. On opening the door, I hobbled on through; the light that appeared around the crack of the door was now gone, and I was once again standing in total darkness. Quietly shutting the door behind myself, I tried to feel with outstretched hands what sort of room that I was now in; but I could feel nothing in any direction, not even a wall or another door. Cautiously taking very small steps, I felt a slight breeze blowing gently across my face. Momentarily, the darkness that had cloaked my person was interrupted by a flicker of light from above myself; looking up, I was astonished to see light intermittently breaking on through the black sky; I then painfully realised, that after all my efforts I had stupidly entered the small window of an

outside toilet and was now   back outside. I was definitely not a happy person. Shamefully, I decided to call it a
night just as the light faded back into total darkness.
Stepping forward away from the house approximately four
feet into the blackness of the night, I fell face down over a
little pointed wooden garden fence, that stood approximately six inches in height. Falling over this little fence did
not help my already bruised and strained leg. I now had
only one thought within my head, and that was to get
myself the hell out of there before I had given myself
another injury. Picking myself up off the ground, I hobbled
very carefully and slowly with both my arms outstretched
to search for the front gate that led back on to the pavement
outside; finding the gate, I entered out on to the pavement.
My mission was disgracefully aborted without honours.
Limping back along the road, I found my friend patiently
waiting upon the corner of the street; on seeing him, he
asked, 'How did you get on?'

I replied, 'Forget it! The taxi-driver must have sold it.'
My friend never did get his radio back.

The Leap in the Air

A few years ago I tried to help a friend to get back his radio that was stolen from him by deception. The person who had stolen the radio was a taxi-driver, who was then known to be into tax evasion and other criminal activities. I failed to retrieve the stolen radio for my friend as I had not fully accomplished my mission at that time.

Four weeks after my failed mission, my friend asked me again to help him retrieve from the same taxi-driver a small lawn-mower, that was also stolen upon that very same day as his radio. Having this second chance to prove my abilities, and to save face upon the failure of my first mission, I agreed to help him. The stolen lawn-mower was situated within a shed at the bottom of the taxi-driver's garden. As before, it was a very, very dark night, with very little street lighting to see my way.

My plan of action was once again in motion. The only way that one could get to the taxi-driver's garden shed where the lawn-mower was being held captive, without being seen, was by jumping over the fences of two neigh-bouring gardens. I told my friend, as before, to wait down the road and out of sight of prying eyes. Unlike before, I had to go past the front of the taxi-driver's house, along the pavement, then to turn left into a cul-de-sac, where his neighbours' gardens were situated. The dividing fencing upon all the gardens were the typical council-type fencing with single pointed wood battens, that ran the full length of each garden; the fences were approximately four feet in height, and were very sturdy. My mission was now in progress. On entering over the first fence from the pavement in the cul-de-sac by leap-frogging, I found myself to be in a bed of flowers; standing up from my crouching position, I then walked across the dark and shadowy garden to the next dividing fence. Upon reaching the next fence, I again leap-frogged over. As I was in mid-air, I found it almost impossible to see below myself through the darkness of the night; luckily, I landed blindly in a vegetable patch, and I felt a sense of relief upon my safe return to earth. Hitting the soft ground with a thud, and with my heels also hitting up against my own backside, had left an impression of my shoes deep within the soil. Standing up once again from my crouching position, I then crossed the second garden to find the next dividing fence. On reaching the next fence, I once again placed myself into readiness for my next leap-frog over. Once I had entered into the next garden, I had only to gain access into the taxi-driver's prison shed to retrieve the captive lawn-mower. Again leap-frogging over the last fence into the blackness of the night, I landed again with my backside making contact with the heels of my shoes; as I did so, a garden bamboo cane went four inches straight up my arse. From my crouching position, I shot straight up into the air. I was not a happy person. My mission was immediately aborted once again.

Painfully, I made my way back across the gardens to my starting point without leap-frogging the fences. On reaching the pavement in the cul-de-sac, I painfully limped back down the poorly-lit road whilst holding my arse to look for my friend. On finding my friend further along the road, he peered into the dimly-lit road as I limped towards him to see if I was in possession of the lawn-mower. Seeing that I was not, he just stood there upon the pavement without uttering a word. I could see that my friend had a look of disappointment about his face, as he again looked into my empty hands. I was now stood facing him whilst holding my backside with both hands, the pain was immense. As he was about to speak; I very quickly said, 'Forget it! Don't ask, don't say a word! Just get yourself another lawn-mower!'

Two weeks later, my backside was still very sore. It will take a few more weeks for my arse to forget that it had its very own break-in. My friend never did ask me to help him again; I don't know why. But if there's anyone out there, with similar problems to my friend, and would like to hire a professional burglar to go on a special mission, then take a look in the *Yellow Pages*.

The Clown

In the Seventies there were a large number of men who had gotten themselves into the rage of the century to have an afro-type hair-style. The afro hair-style was a mass of tight curls ornamentally arranged upon the head, by using a number of small plastic curlers. For men to have curlers stuck upon their heads in those days was not very manly. Most men in the old days who wanted the afro hair-style would have it applied to themselves behind closed doors, and away from embarrassing prying eyes. When the man wore the afro look, he would hope that the ordinary person in the street would look upon the new hair-style as being natural. I know, because I was one of those men. One evening in the Seventies my sister arrived at my home to rearrange my wife's hair-do. Whilst my sister was sorting out the wife's hair, I sat down to watch the television. As time passed, the work on my wife's head was completed. My sister looked to me, as I sat quietly minding my own business watching the television. Then suddenly, without warning, my sister grabbed at my arm and pulled me out from my comfortable armchair. She then pushed me back down upon a nearby small wooden chair with a mischievous smile; I looked to her with a look of surprise as she said, 'Stay just where you are, I'm going to try and sort out the mess upon your head.'

Knowing that my hair was a mess, I let her have her wicked way, as I continued to watch the television from my new sitting position. My sister unexpectedly pushed my head down into a bowl of water, to wash and shampoo it. The bowl was conveniently placed upon another wooden chair beside the seat that I was forcibly sat upon. As she washed my hair, I was still trying to watch the television. I was not a happy person. After washing my hair, and then violently rubbing the hair dry with a towel, my sister then told me to sit very still, whilst she went about rearranging my hair for the new look. My sister told me that she was going to make my hair look curly. In order to have a little peace and quiet, I agreed to let her have her little bit of fun, but only on the condition that the front door was locked, and that I was not at home to any other person who happened to drop by. On locking the front door, my sister started about my head with the comb and lots of curlers.

Upon my big nose was a very large spot, which had doubled the size of my nose. The reason why my nose was in this inflamed condition was quite simply because I had pulled out a nose hair the night before; it did look a sight. There I now was, sat upon a chair with a head full of curlers, and a very big red nose. My sister and my wife fell about laughing as they looked upon the sight before them. Their laughing become uncontrollable as their eyes filled with tears. I had given up trying to watch the television, and I was still without a doubt, not a happy person.

The next day, after getting up from a good night's sleep with my hair now very curly, and my nose larger and redder then before I sent my wife laughing once again hysterically to the floor. She, whilst trying to compose herself, remarked that I looked like one of the Marx Brothers; the Marx Brother to whom she was referring was the one who could not speak and held within his hand a bicycle horn; the bicycle horn, as most of us already know, was used to communicate by honking. Now very annoyed by my wife's continuous laughing at the sight of myself, I ventured on out into the rear garden, via the back door of the house, to get a little peace and quiet. Around the perimeter of my garden, I had previously erected a wooden six-foot trellis fence. Whilst walking around my garden with my blond hair now full of curls, and this great big red abnormal Roman nose, I could hear my neighbour mowing his lawn next door. Peering over a part of the fencing by standing upon a dustbin, I could plainly see the neighbour, who was also my friend, going up and down in his own garden with the lawn-mower. Peering over with my red nose resting on the fence like Chad, and my blond curls slightly blowing in the breeze, I shouted, 'Hoy!' My neighbour stopped what he was doing to look up to see who was calling him; on looking up in my direction, he could see only the top of my curly blond head and a very large glowing red nose peering back down at him from over the fence. My friend immediately fell to the ground in fits of laughter. He was laughing so much, he lay doubled up upon his side in agony upon the grass. Holding tight his stomach with both hands, my friend found that he could not get up off the ground.

From the rear window of his own home, his wife could see that her husband was laid upon the lawn and in difficulties; on seeing that her husband was in some sort of trouble, she ran out to help him. Not knowing what was really wrong with him, she very quickly knelt down to attend to his possible needs. Upon kneeling down to attend to her husband, she simultaneously looked up to where I was still peering over the fence at them both. On sighting me, she too rolled with laughter upon the lawn. As she laughed with tears running down her own face, she tried in vain to get her husband up from off the ground. Her husband was also still laughing with the tears streaming down his face whilst holding his own stomach in pain. Every time he laughed, it only made the pain worse. Their eldest son then came out of the house to see what the commotion was all about. Seeing the problem, the son and his mother carried my friend back into the house away from the sight of myself upon the fencing. The son then called in the doctor.

When the doctor arrived, he examined my friend whilst he laid upon the settee within the rear room, which looked back out on to the garden. I could see clearly what was happening from the top of the fencing looking back down into their living-room through the open French windows. The doctor was trying very hard to stop my friend laughing, whilst under examination. My neighbour's garden had a cul-de-sac to one side of it; people passing by could hear my friend laughing hysterically. As he lay there upon the sofa, with a cushion drenched with tears beneath his head, the doctor finally managed to get a result from his examination. The doctor found that my friend had in fact burst three blood vessels in the pit of his stomach. He then gave to my friend's wife and son a strict and direct order; that they must at all cost keep him away from his next-door neighbour. The doctor, in his own words, considered that I was dangerous. My friend was off work for three days after that. He was a happy person.

I saw on the news recently that a comic, believe it or not, was wanted for murder; he was on the run from the police after a spectator at his show died of laughter. The spectator, a woman, died of a heart attack, brought on by her own laughter. When the woman was in actual pain from the laughing, the comic had added unknowingly to her pain by making faces at her. She had then collapsed and died within the audience. The last report was that the police were still in pursuit of her killer. After you have read my own true story above, I can only say one thing: I am a lucky person. What has happened to this American comic could have happened to me. She was a happy woman.

The Mormons

A few years ago, upon one hot summer's day, I had somehow to move my Ford Transit pick-up truck from off the
road, and into my back garden for repairs.

My house was the second from the end on a line of
other houses. There was no side access to the rear of my
own garden. The repairs to the chassis of this pick-up truck
could not be done upon the road. The rear garden of my
home was the most suitable place to work for the removal
and repair of the rear transporting box. The only possible
way that I could drive this truck into the rear of my garden
was to drive it around the corner into a cul-de-sac, and
across my neighbour's garden, then on into my own
garden. With my neighbour's permission, I had done just
that. After taking down my neighbour's four feet high
fencing that separated his garden from the pavement, I
drove my Ford Transit truck on to the pavement, across his
lawn, until I came against my own dividing garden fence.
After taking down a part of my own four feet high fencing,
I then drove the Ford Transit pick-up on through into my
own garden. On parking it, I then set about replacing both
my fencing, and that of the neighbours.

I had been working upon the rear of this Ford Transit
for approximately six weeks; as it neared completion, a very
funny and unexpected thing occurred. Whilst I was out in
the rear garden replacing the last few remaining bolts that
held tight the transporting box upon the rear chassis of the
Ford Transit, I heard a very loud banging coming from the

front door of my house. Covered in grease, with spanner in hand, I walked up the garden, then into the house to answer the front door. As I reached the front door from inside the house, the door knocker again banged heavily; it was a wonder that whoever it was knocking on the door had not knocked the door completely off its hinges; I wasn't a happy person.

On opening the front door, I saw two men; one black, and one white. 'What do you want?' I asked in anger.

'Do you believe in God?' asked the white man with a hopeful look about his face.

Looking at them both, I replied, 'Look! I am not knocking your religion as hard as you have been knocking on my door; it's just that to me, seeing is believing, and I am a busy man.'

The white Mormon then asked, 'Do you feel warm?'

I then looked at him with curiosity and replied, 'Er, yes! Why do you ask?'

'Do you know why you feel warm?' asked the white Mormon.

'You tell me!' I answered in abrupt impatience.

'It's that sun up there, that's why you feel warm,' said the white Mormon, pointing in the direction of the bright yellow sun.

'Is it!' I replied, in an uninterested manner.

'Do you know who put the sun there?' asked the white Mormon with a smile.

'No! Do you?' I asked sarcastically.

'Yes! God put it there,' the white Mormon replied with an even bigger smile.

'Did you see him put it there?' I asked, whilst patiently glancing at my watch.

The white Mormon then went on to say, 'God creates miracles; when one prays, all sorts of weird and wonderful things happens; if you were to pray, and pray, and pray, and pray, the unbelievable is sure to happen; God makes life worth living,' he added with a contented smile.

After the white Mormon had said his piece, I looked at the two of them together and said, 'Look! I don't want to appear rude, but I can't stay here all day talking to you, I have work to do.'

The white Mormon then replied with a smile, 'Yes! I understand, I'm sorry to have held you up, good day.'

The two Mormons turned to walk back out of my front gate, and on to the pavement outside.

Once they had both gone from the front gate and out of my sight, I shut tight the door. I then returned to the rear garden to finish what I was doing. As I picked up a bolt, I could see the two Mormons walking along the pavement, into the cul-de-sac alongside my neighbour's fence.

Moments later, I looked to the end of my garden at the two Mormons, who were now knocking upon the front door of a house; throwing down the spanner, I walked down to the very bottom of my garden to where a dividing hedge was situated. Peering through a hole in the hedge at the two Mormons, I shouted, 'Hoy! They are not in, they are on holiday.'

'Oh! Thanks,' came the reply. They both then left the garden through an entrance gate. On closing the gate, they proceeded to leave the cul-de-sac. The Mormons then walked back alongside my neighbour's fence in order to get back on to the main road, whilst I walked back to the truck to finish the job that I was doing. As I was about to continue with my work, I could hear someone shouting, 'Excuse me! I say! Excuse me!'

Looking up from my place of work in the direction of the shouting, I could see the two Mormons standing and shouting over to me, from within the cul-de-sac. 'Excuse me!' came the shout once again. As I looked at them both, the white Mormon waved his hand in the air to make sure that he had my full attention.

'What do you want?' I asked in a fed up voice.

The white Mormon then shouted, 'My colleague and I were wondering how on earth you got that truck into your back garden? Would you mind telling us how you did that?'

After the white Mormon had finished asking me with a bewildered look upon his face, I looked down to the base of the fences; I could then see why they had asked. The grass had re-grown along the border line at the base of both fences. Looking at the fences, one would never have thought that the fences at one time had been removed; for the grass at the base of the fences was now quite long. After looking at the grass at the base of the fences, I then looked back up in the direction of the two Mormons, who were still waiting for my reply; I answered by shouting back to them both, 'You will not believe me, if I tell you!'

Both the Mormons looked at each other, then back to me, as the white Mormon shouted over, 'Well, try us!'

I replied, 'Okay! If you must know I will tell you; but you may not believe me.'

'Try us!' shouted the white Mormon once again.

'Well okay, here's what happened; I had this truck parked on the road to the front of my house, and I was standing beside it, thinking to myself, how am I going to get this truck into the rear of my garden? And then it came to me!' As I was talking, I could see that the two Mormons were very intrigued by what I was saying, so I continued, 'As I stood beside my truck, I placed my hands together and started to pray, and pray, and pray, and pray, and I prayed! I told you, you won't believe me.'

'Yes! Yes! Please do carry on!' shouted the white Mormon with great interest in what I was saying, leaning upon my neighbour's fence.

Looking at them both, I knew that I had them both well and truly hooked. My timing was perfect. I then looked at them both, as I continued with my story, describing what happened with the use of my hands. 'Well! As I stood there by my truck praying, a miracle occurred. Lo and behold, the truck very slowly lifted itself from off the road, I watched in amazement as my truck started to float up into the air, then out of sight over the roof-tops. Seeing this miracle, I ran into my house to get to the rear garden; as I reached the rear garden, the truck had slowly descended down from over the roof-tops into the garden; it landed like a feather, ever so lightly! Then it bounced a little before finally resting upon the grass. There you have it gentlemen, that's how the truck got into my garden.'

After telling this true story to the two Mormons, I could see the white Mormon still leaning upon the fence thinking about what I had just said. Suddenly he went into a rage, then stormed off down the road. He wasn't a happy person. The black Mormon, who had not spoken at any time, was now laid upon the pavement in fits of laughter; he was hysterical. Seeing him laid upon the pavement laughing the way that he was, was a sight in itself! He was a very happy person. His white colleague had gone off in a huff, and left him rolling about the pavement. Picking himself up off the pavement, still in fits of laughter, the black Mormon stumbled off to find his mate. As he did so, he wiped away the tears from his eyes with the cuff of his coat. I never did see the pair of them again.

When the truck was completed, I removed the two fences in order to get the truck back out and on to the road. I then very quickly replaced the fencing, just in case they decided to return.

The Jam Butty

When I was nine years old, I used to sit and play in my cousin's house next door. One day, I can recall that my cousin, who was a year older than I, was sitting down eating a jam butty whilst watching television. Sat down almost beside him drinking tea was the lodger. The lodger was a little old blind lady, who in height was approximately four foot nothing. This little old lady always wore inside and outside, winter and summer, a very big black long heavy coat, with a flat black hat, that was seemingly perched upon her frail grey old head in an unsettled manner. Wherever she was situated within the family's relaxing front room after meals, her white cane was always at hand. Looking at this little old lady reminded me of that famous cartoon character that was portrayed in Giles's pre-war comic books; I would go as far as to say that the cartoon character portrayed in these comic books could have been copied from her.

This little old blind women hated my cousin, and she often let him know it. While my cousin was about to start eating a second slice of bread that was overladen with jam, the little old lady spat at my cousin for no reason at all. My cousin immediately reacted by slamming his slice of bread and jam straight into the face of the little old lady. I fell about laughing. Moments later, an argument erupted between my cousin, his mother, and the little old blind lady. Seeing the argument growing by the second, I got up from my chair and left the room in tears of laughter.

I then went back to my own home next door. Being nine years of age, I was quite taken by what my cousin had just done to the little old blind lady; I was in fact, hysterical. Hopping over a little dividing wall to the front of the two houses, I walked on in, through the already open front door of my own home, down the passage-way, into the living-room.

Walking through the living-room, I had to pass by my mother, who was sat by the fire, and my godmother, who was sat on the edge of a very big heavy wooden dinner-table. My godmother was reminiscing with my dear old mum about the golden years. Passing my dear old mum and godmother, I entered another room; the scullery, where the foodstuff was kept. Taking out a loaf of uncut bread from the old wooden wire-meshed meat safe, I cut off a single slice of white bread; I then adorned the slice with a half-pot of home-made strawberry jam. Placing the slice of bread with its mountain of jam on the flat of my hand, I went back into the living-room, to where my mother and godmother were still reminiscing. I walked straight up to my godmother, and let fly the jam butty straight into her face whilst she was still sitting at the big dinner-table; she was not a happy person. Stepping back from the jam butty that was now stuck fast to my god-mother's face, I could just see half an eye peering back at me through one of her glass lenses, half covered by jam.

For a moment, apart from my laughter, there was a deadly silence; then my mother got up out of her chair by the fireside, and asked, as she gave me the thrashing of my life, 'What did you do that for?'

I replied, 'Because I thought it was funny! Cousin Pete did the same to the little old blind lady,' I added, with tears of pain mixed with tears of laughter.

With that, my mother left the room to go next door to see her sister, this being my auntie and my cousin's mum.

She was closely followed by my godmother and then myself to the pavement outside; for some reason or another, my mother, my godmother, my auntie and the little old blind lady were now all outside on the pavement doing a lot of shouting.

As I stood there upon the pavement watching, I decided for my own safety to move away from what could turn into a full-scale battle. As the shouting got more and more heated, I dived into a nearby yellow privet hedge to escape a further battering.

Entering the privet hedge head first I found that I was not alone. Looking about myself, I found my cousin within the hedge snivelling from the back of his mother's hand. Peering out from amongst the leaves of the hedge, we could both see the little old blind lady and my godmother, who both still had jam adorning their faces, whilst arguing with my mother and my cousin's mum. We both looked at each other in silence with tears upon the cheeks of our faces; then burst out laughing, holding our sticky fingers over our mouths to quiet the noise.

The Second Warning

A few years ago, when I was a lorry driver, an extraordinary, unexpected occurrence occurred while I was on hire to a building site. The building site, being just one of my many different assignments, was situated in the Botley area of Southampton. The type of lorry that I was driving at that time was a five-yard tipper. In those days, when I was very much younger, I found it to be very difficult to get out of bed in the morning; I was nearly always late on site; how I managed to hold on to this type of employment over the years, I will never know. This story begins here, on what was supposed to have been an early-morning arrival at the building site.

I was supposed to have been on the building site at eight in the morning; but this was not to be! I had left the base rather late, and arrived at the building site in Botley half an hour later than scheduled. Upon my arrival, I found that the site foreman, was not amused by my lateness; but lucky me, I was able to smooth over my lateness with an elaborate lie.

For a summer's day, it was very cold, cloudy and windy; the sun, which appeared spasmodically between the clouds, was very dismal. As a lorry driver, I had to wear extra clothing to keep out the cold as winter neared; unlike today, most lorries had no heaters to keep one warm. Upon my arrival, I could see that there was quite a lot of site clearance being undertaken by other contractors; some parts of the building site had been totally flattened by bulldozers in order to make way for the erection of new houses. I myself was on hire to this building site for the relocation of top soil; the top soil was to be transported from one end of the site to a compound, which was situated at the far end of the building site, for stockpiling. I was supposed to have been on contract hire to this building site for the whole day upon my arrival; but because of the extraordinary unexpected phenomenon that was to follow, upon my parking at the site, made it impossible for me to do so. I was situated upon that building site for one hour only; it was an hour in my life that I will never forget. Within that one hour, the first part of my extraordinary phenomenon had occurred; a phenomenon that would boggle one's imagination.

This strange phenomenon happened after I had jumped out from my lorry to the ground. After landing on the ground beside the front wheel, the foreman approached me with the instructions of the day. I was instructed to have my lorry loaded with the top soil by a JCB; this being an earth-moving machine. After the foreman had given to me my instructions, I replied, 'Right!'

I then turned to face the open cab door, to enter the cab. At this point in the story, it is necessary to explain the following movements to you; for this is when this strange but true phenomenon took place.

On stretching up, I held on to the inside handle upon the cab door with my right hand. I then placed my left foot upon a step-up, which was situated on the outside, just below the left-hand side of the driver's door; to complete the manoeuvre into the cab, I had to then place my left hand tightly on to another specially adapted handle, situated upon the outside cab's structure above my head to the left; I was now ready to pull myself further on up into the cab, thus leaving my right foot, the last to leave the ground upon that final upward pull into the cab.

Just as my right foot had left the ground upon that final

upward pull, the ground beneath my right boot had collapsed from under it.

Holding on to the outside cab handle with my left hand, and the inside door handle with my right hand, I momentarily froze; it was as if time itself had stopped still as my own person and one leg hung motionless above the hole beneath myself.

Frozen in time, I, as if in slow motion, looked back down to where my right boot was still dangling above the deep black hole, and to where the ground once was. In my state of disbelief as to what had just happened, whilst looking back down to where my right boot had just been; I could feel the sweat upon my brow running down the cheeks of my face; it was like looking back down into deep space. There was nothing there.

On finally completing my entry back into the cab of the lorry, I sat down upon the driving seat with sweat streaming down both cheeks of my face and on to my lap.

After a moment or two, I looked back down from the open cab door to where the foreman was still situated. The foreman, who had been watching me from the beginning, was now himself stood gazing with disbelief into the big black hole that was situated just below the cab door. He too could not believe what had just happened, and what he was now looking down upon. 'Well I never! What the hell is that doing there?' the foreman asked with a look of amazement upon his now white face.

Looking back down upon him from the cab, I asked, *'What the fuck is it?'*

The site foreman replied, 'It looks like an old well! I can't even see the bottom; as far as I can make out, it shouldn't be there.'

With the sweat still running down my face, I restarted the engine of the tipper lorry. Slamming tight the cab door, I then looked out and down from the open cab window to where the foreman was still standing; from my sitting position, I could see that he too was in a conundrum over the mysterious hole. I then said, 'That's it! I'm off.'

The foreman just stood there, as if lost for words; he then stood and watched, as I drove off the building site, on to the road, and then into the direction of my home base.

On my return back to base, I had to explain to my boss why I had left the building site; he was not a happy person. After I told him of my ordeal, he sent back to the building site a replacement driver and lorry, whilst I myself was given a new assignment for the remainder of the day.

Two days had now passed since my ordeal, and I was content working on another site; but it was short-lived. On my return back to base after a day's work, I was ordered to return to the building site in Botley, for an eight o'clock start that following morning; now I was not a happy person. Having to do as I was told, the following morning I returned to the building site in Botley as ordered, ten minutes late as usual. On re-entering the building site, I could see the foreman standing and waiting for my arrival. He uttered not a word about my lateness; in fact, he was quite pleasant. 'All right?' he asked with a smile; I replied only with a nod of the head as I looked down at him from the cab window. He then said, with a smile, 'I have had the surveyors out here searching for more of them holes; they told me that it was an old well, and they have now given it the all-clear,' he finished with confidence.

'What sort of well was it?' I asked.

'It was an old Roman well,' replied the foreman; 'we had to back-fill the well with brick rubble, then finish it off with a whole lorry-load of wet concrete; it was surprisingly deep,' again the foreman added with yet another forced smile.

I just sat there looking down at him from the inside cab, as he then stepped a little nearer to the front wheel of the lorry that was situated just below the cab door. I then looked up to the moving vehicles that were now running the top soil about the site. The day was cold and dismal again, and I was now wearing an army camouflage jacket to help keep out the cold; this army camouflage jacket, unbeknown to myself at that time, was to save my life within the next few moments. I was now about to receive the second part of the strange phenomenon that I had encountered upon my last short visit to this building site.

After looking at the vehicles moving about the site, I looked back down to the foreman as he asked, 'Will you please leave the lorry there, and follow me; I will then show you what I want you to do today.' He then walked a little further away from the tipper lorry, then stopped, as if to be waiting for me.

As the foreman walked away from the front wheel of the tipper lorry, I simultaneously opened the cab door to jump out; it was at this point in time that the strange extraordinary unexpected occurrence happened. It was something that went against all odds, the unbelievable. As I made that jump from the cab of the tipper lorry to the ground, the back of my army camouflage jacket caught on to the inner handle of the open cab door whilst I was still in mid-air upon that downward jump. The whole of my body came to a sudden stop with a jerk, just as the toe of my right boot slightly touched the ground below; as the toe of my right boot touched the ground, an extraordinary, unexpected, strange phenomenon once again entered my very charmed life. The ground once again opened up beneath myself; another deep black hole had mysteriously appeared directly below my now hanging body.

On seeing this second hole beneath myself, I, with an unnaturally quick reflex, that was without a doubt faster then the speed of light, grabbed for the nearest thing to hand; as the cab door swung to and fro with the movement of my own body weight, I was able to reach out and grab at the very long protruding mirror arm that was attached to the front of the cab. I then simultaneously blindly stretched out my right arm, to try and find something else to hold on to; but to no avail. I was too far away from the cab itself. To make my predicament worse, a wind had slowly started to materialise. The wind fought against me with the added movement of my own body weight upon the cab door, forcing the door and myself to sway to and fro together, time and time again. As the door and myself closed inwards towards the frame of the open cab, the wind would again force the cab door and myself back out against the wing of the lorry. I was like a puppet on a string with nowhere to go. Having the back of my coat held fast upon the unseen handle behind had forced my view towards the open building site as I floated in mid-air. Looking down and about to understand more fully my present situation, I let go of the mirror arm that I had held on to through the open window of the cab door, just as the door blew back shut; simultaneously I grabbed at the cab roof with both hands, just as I was also able to place a foothold on the seat within the cab in front of myself.

Upon grabbing the slippery, smooth outside edge of the cab roof with two hands, and now having a firm foothold upon the seat within, I looked back down to see where the foreman was situated. He was but a stone's throw away; I could see that he was just standing and watching my every move, but this time with open mouth; he was of no help and totally useless in my predicament. I could also plainly see the deep black open mouth of the hole beneath myself, as if it were a monster waiting to swallow me up for ever upon one slip from my coat hanger. Now facing and touching the cab driving seat with both feet, I had some-how, and without letting go of the cab's slippery roof, to unhook the rear of my camouflage jacket from the unseen handle to the back of myself. Pushing both my feet down upon the seat together with my hold upon the edge of the cab roof, I was able to set myself free by pushing and pulling myself up and off the handle. The moment that I was free of the handle, I grabbed for the steering wheel with my right hand, to pull myself on into the cab, just as my other hand slipped off the cab roof. On my release, the cab door swung more freely in both directions, as the wind got a little angrier. I sighed with relief as I entered freedom and safety.

Slamming tight the cab door as before, I once again looked back down at the foreman through the open cab window; I could see him standing and looking into the deep black hole as he had done previously upon my first strange encounter. He stood staring in total disbelief at the second hole's unexpected and untimely appearance. The foreman looked back up at me just as I restarted the tipper lorry's engine; for the few moments that followed, he did not utter a word.

I then said, 'That's it! I'm off!'

The foreman suddenly replied in an angry voice, 'You can't do that!'

I looked at him as the lorry slowly nudged on past him, and replied, 'Can't I! You just watch me.'

I then pointed out to him that this was my second warning, and that there was not going to be a third. Picking up a little more speed, I then drove away from the building site for the very last time, and returned to base.

The Wrong Car

A few years ago I owned a blue Ford Cortina car. One summer's day, (this being a Saturday afternoon), I drove my car downtown into the city of Southampton to do a little shopping. In the town I parked my car outside what was then 'Owens and Owens'. Owens and Owens was a very big clothing superstore. To find a parking space in town on a Saturday afternoon was not an easy task; but as luck would have it, I found a parking space just outside the Owens and Owens superstore upon the road, between a line of other parked cars; I parked my car in a small gap with careful consideration for the other vehicles already parked to my front and rear. After I had parked the car, I had only a few steps to walk before entering the big clothing store.

I was shopping within the store for approximately ten minutes before returning to my parked car at the kerbside. On my return to the car, I started up the engine, and then proceeded to move on out from the line of cars to get into the flow of the passing traffic; as I pulled out from the line of tightly parked cars, I noticed upon the dashboard a load of mixed rubbish, that ran the whole length of the dashboard to the base of the windscreen. Looking at the rubbish, my first thoughts were that someone was playing a game with me; my second thoughts were that whoever it was had seen me park the car at the roadside. I was confident that it was someone playing some sort of practical joke upon me. But then, I said to myself, 'Wait a minute, how could that have happened; the door was locked.' I wasn't a happy person. Suddenly stopping the car in the middle of the road just as I had pulled out from the parking space, I looked once again at the unrecognisable rubbish that lined the dashboard. I felt that there was something not quite right about the car; but what? I was not too sure. The road behind being clear of moving traffic, I reversed the car back into the parking space. On re-parking the car, I stepped out. Standing upon the pavement after alighting from the vehicle, I slammed shut the door; I then looked about the car as I stood upon the pavement in bewilderment.

The car looked like mine; in fact, I was certain it was mine. The car was the same colour and looked to be of the right year, even the car aerial looked about right; it was an old wire coat hanger. Again I opened the car door to inspect the interior of the car and the rubbish upon the dashboard. The car interior was the right colour; but no! The rubbish was definitely not mine. Life would have been a little simpler for myself if only I had remembered the registration number of the car. But, as we all know, life is not always that simple; not every person can remember the registration number of his or her own car. After taking my keys back out from the ignition, I once again shut the car door. Stepping back and away from the car on the pavement with my hands upon my hips, I looked into the direction that the blue Cortina's headlights were facing, to look at the car in front; I then looked to the rear of the blue Cortina; both were of a different make and colour. I then looked at the blue Cortina with the rubbish lined upon the dashboard; my thoughts were that this car must be mine. I then said to myself, as I turned my head in the direction of the superstore, and then once again back to the blue Cortina, 'This blue Cortina looked as if it was parked in the same way that I had parked mine; so this one has to be mine.'

After standing and looking at the blue Cortina at the kerbside with confused thoughts, I then stepped backwards upon the pavement away from the car to enable myself to look further up the road to the left, this being once again in the same direction that the front headlights of the blue Cortina was facing. Upon stepping back upon the pavement to look further up the road, I could then plainly see another blue car. This blue car was two cars further along the line. On inspecting the other blue car, I could see that it was another Cortina; inspecting this car further, I discovered that this car was truly mine. Very quickly, I opened the car door, and re-entered my own car. Upon ignition, I drove off as fast as I could possibly go. I have often wondered what the other car owner would have said or done if he had actually caught me driving away his car.

The Portuguese Man-of-War

At the age of fifteen I left school to start my first job as a mill boy in a timber yard; the timber yard, Montague L. Meyer's, was situated within the Great Western Docks of Southampton. Montague L. Meyer's was one of the biggest timber yards around at that time. In the hot summer months of August, all the mill boys used to go swimming off the quayside in the dinner hour. In those days I was not a very good swimmer; the only type of swimming that I was able to do when I was a nipper was the doggy paddle. This meant that I could only swim in a place of safety. In the Southampton Docks, there was an old iron ladder that was fixed firmly to the wall face of the quayside; this ladder was ideal for the likes of myself to enter the water with safety. Sea-going people used to use this iron ladder to enter or alight small crafts, by stepping down from the top quayside to the water below.

Upon one hot summer's day, I and all the other mill boys who worked together in the big timber sheds, were all sitting in the tea room listening to the news on the radio, whilst having our ten o'clock morning break. The radio announced that because of all the unusual hot weather that we were having, dangerous Portuguese man-of-war jellyfish had entered into our waters. The newspapers and the radio also stated that these jellyfish could inflict unsightly wounds or even death upon a person. The public in general were warned not to go swimming in the sea, as there could be unmeasurable consequences.

As immature lads we laughed and cracked jokes over the incoming reports, in a very childish manner; but for some unknown reason, I had the thought of those giant jellyfish in the back of my mind for the remainder of that morning.

Dinner time was now upon us, and the thoughts of the jellyfish to the back of my mind had now disappeared. Nine mill boys, including myself, left the timber yard to take the four minutes' walk to the quayside for a midday swim. On reaching the quayside, some of the mill hands were jumping into the water with nothing on; I myself was one of them. Others had put woollen hand-knitted bathers on; bathers in those days were mostly made by one's parents. When the wool got wet, the weight of the water used to pull them back down below their knees, as they jumped back into the water from the quayside. Approximately ten yards further away from the others, I had found one of those iron ladders. Normally, I would have climbed down the iron ladder; but this time, I jumped into the sea from off the top of the quayside. Without a stitch of clothing on, I made one almighty splash into the murky water below disappearing from sight; upon re-surfacing, I felt something huge clamping itself on to my back then wrapping itself tightly around my naked body. Whatever it was, it had no intentions on letting me go. It scared the shit out of me, as I splashed about the surface with this unseen thing refusing to leave my person.

The heavily weighted unseen thing upon my back was pulling me back down under the surface; I could hardly move as I strained to do the doggy paddle. I stretched my head out of the water as far as it could possibly go, in order to breathe above the surface of the sea. In my struggle to survive, I suddenly remembered the giant Portuguese man-of-war jellyfish; I was now splashing about the water in an uncontrollable frenzied manner. Whatever I had upon my back was doing its utmost to stop me surfacing. Now doing fifty knots to the inch with my doggy paddling, I tried desperately to reach the iron ladder that was approximately one yard away. Every time I got a little nearer to the ladder with an outstretched grasping hand, this slimy-feeling thing upon my back kept forcing me back down under the deep water. Using all the strength that I could muster, I could from time to time steal a gulp of fresh air whenever my head was permitted to surface. Manoeuvring nearer to the iron ladder in my struggle for survival, with my strength almost gone, I was finally able to grab the bottom rung with an outstretched hand, just as this slimy unseen thing upon my back tried to force me under the water for the very last time.

On successfully grabbing the bottom rung of the ladder with my last and final grab upon the bottom rung, I managed to raise my head and the unseen slimy mass upon my back slightly up the ladder. The more I tried to pull myself further up on to the second rung; the heavier this thing on my back had become. I could feel what appeared to be very long tentacles wrapping themselves more tightly around my naked waist as I strained to climb the ladder a little further. The tentacles were now affecting my breathing; I was now one third up the iron ladder. I pulled my naked body tight into the rungs of the ladder as I made my climb upwards to stop the weight of this thing upon my back pulling me back off; I tried to turn my head to the left of myself to see what it was upon my back, but to no avail. I could feel a mountain of water cascading down from off the thing upon my back, to the backs of my legs, as I slid my body further up the iron ladder. My whole body strength was now almost gone. The top of the ladder looked as if it were miles away as I continued to slowly slide my naked body up the iron ladder to reach the half-way mark. Holding my naked body tight into the ladder whilst pausing for a moment to catch my breath, with my left cheek pressed against an iron rung, I glanced back down to look at the green seaweed-stained quayside wall below; I then strained my distorted and tired body, to try and see what was wrapped around the front of my waist, by nervously releasing my tensed grip upon the ladder, then slightly pushing my body outwards; but I could not see past my own chest. The weight of this thing upon my back was pulling the top half of my body outwards, further away from the ladder as my knees were joined to the rungs to help my arms take the strain. I pulled my naked body back in tight to the ladder for fear of the weight pulling me off. Whilst still holding firmly to the iron ladder, with my left cheek once again pressed tightly into the iron rung, I viewed the lapping water below; to my horror, I could see a single Portuguese man-of-war bobbing about the waves at the base of the green-stained seaweed wall.

Resting my forehead upon a rung of the ladder, I tried to take in the reality of it all. It was like a living dream, a dream with no ending; time was at a standstill, I did not know how long I had been holding on to the ladder. It seemed like hours. After resting my forehead upon the rung of the ladder for a few moments, I again looked back down to the water below. Surprisingly, I could now see that the Portuguese men-of-war were now in abundance. A new strength surged throughout my body to force both the combined weight of myself and the thing upon my back further up the ladder. As I pushed forever forward, I could hear the other mill hands further along the quayside enjoying themselves. My throat was too dry to cry out. Slowly, I continued to pull myself skyward; I was now almost to the top of the ladder. I could see in my mind's eye my whole life flashing by before me. The last few iron rungs seemed yards apart, I did not think that I was going to make the top of the ladder. As I finally neared the top, I tried once again to shrug off the clammy object held fast to my back and around my waist; but, as before, it resisted all attempts to be shaken loose.

As my head slowly emerged above the quayside from the top of the iron ladder, I could see, further along the quayside, all the other mill boys getting themselves dressed and ready to leave. This one hour for a dinner break was, without a doubt, the longest hour that I had ever known. On reaching the top of the iron ladder; I stood balancing upon the second rung from the top, whilst holding the top rung with both hands; my bare arse was now arched towards the sun in the clear blue sky. The weight upon my back made me feel very unsteady as I held tight to the top rung. I looked to the concrete surface of the quayside to the front of myself, and then to where other dock workers were now walking about nearby upon the quayside; in full view of my nakedness, I threw my naked person into a forward roll from the ladder, on to the hard concrete surface of the quayside; whilst in that forward roll, the clammy thing clamped upon my back started to release its grip from around my waist. Looking at my stomach whilst in that same forward roll from off the ladder, I could plainly see that it was not a Portuguese man-of-war as I had first thought, but, an entangled mass of seaweed wrapped tightly around my waist; the seaweed had unbuckled itself from around my waist like a belt on contact with the quayside. A great sense of relief befell me, as my eyes looked upon the wet clammy seaweed that almost killed me; I could not believe after all that, it turned out to be a big lump of seaweed. After pulling off the remaining seaweed, I then laid my naked body down upon the concrete to face the sun. As I lay there, with other dock workers looking at me whilst going about their business, I said to myself, God, it's good to be alive.

After a short rest, I stood up to look over the side whence I had just come; whilst putting my clothing back on, I could clearly see over a wide area upon the surface of the sea, an enormous amount of jellyfish, bobbing about the surface. After that memorable day, I never did go swimming in the docks again. To have gotten out of that situation in one piece definitely made me a happy person. On seeing the other mill hands now on their way back to work, I told them of my ordeal. They all laughed at my near-death adventure; they thought it to have been funny. The seaweed wrapped about my body had almost killed me; but on the other hand, it could have saved me from another certain death.

The Dirty Neck

At the age of fourteen I had a very dark sun tan; I only had to be in the sunlight for an hour or two for my entire body to change to golden brown. The longer I stayed in the sunlight, the darker I became. In two weeks, the golden tan would change to an almost black colour. In the old days, kids wore very little clothing in the height of summer. We did not use sun creams in those days; everything was very natural, and in balance with nature. Little did I know that this deep dark natural tan would cause me so much grief upon my return to school soon after the school holidays.

The teachers, for some reason or another on my return to school, had it in for me. I asked some of the teachers why was I always picked upon for no real reason. Their answers were always the same; they told me, that they never pick on any one person for no reason. No matter what the teachers gave me for an answer, I sensed that they were not very truthful in their replies to my question. I had known for a very long time that they were indeed picking upon me; but I could not really prove it until one day in the middle of August, whilst I was sat at my desk undergoing the teaching of technical drawings. The teacher of the day was wandering up and down in between each of the many different rows of desks, with both hands held behind his back. In one of his hands, he held tight a short cane which he was slapping slightly against his own back, as he paced up and down the aisles. Whilst he paced the aisles, he would very quietly and sneakily look over each pupil's shoulder as he moved slowly around the class-room.

Upon this particular day, I felt his presence directly behind myself as I was busy attending to my lesson; the unexpected happened. The teacher not only made me jump, he also showed me up for no real reason in front of the whole class, as he bellowed, *'Johnson! Stand up!'* Upon my standing to face him, he grabbed my shirt collar, then pulled the collar down to expose the rear side of my neck. Holding down the collar, he bellowed, 'Go and wash your dirty, filthy neck!'

The teacher then let go of my collar by jerking his hand up and away from my person, whilst pointing to the class-room door with his other hand, for me to make an exit.

Before leaving, I looked about the class-room to where my classmates were all sneakily trying not to look around from their own desks to see what was going on. Whilst I momentarily stood there with all the colours of the rainbow about my own face, I felt embarrassed and shown up; I could have died right there and then. I wasn't a happy person.

'Out!' shouted the teacher, pointing his finger once again towards the class-room door. On leaving the class-room with my tail between my legs, I went straight to the wash-room; looking into the mirror, I could see nothing wrong with my neck. I could only see the very dark sun tan that adorned the skin upon my neck. Feeling really let down and full of embarrassment by what had happened within the class-room, I glanced down at the wash-basin just as I released my shirt collar to inspect myself within the mirror. Looking down at the wash-basin, I found a half-used cigarette and two matches in a box, that must have been left by a teacher. That was my very first cigarette. After I had finished the half-smoked cigarette, I walked slowly and reluctantly back to the class-room; on reaching the class-room door, I felt a sense of fear returning and running

throughout the whole of my body. Holding tight my breath, I entered the class-room.

On shutting the class-room door behind myself, I looked to the teacher, who was beckoning me with his finger. With further feelings of embarrassment, I immediately walked slowly towards him. On doing so, I could see all my classmates once again trying not to look to see what was going on. With me standing before him, he once again pulled down my shirt collar very low to the base of my neck. The teacher then said, after re-inspecting the back of my neck, in a low voice, 'That's better, now go and sit down.' Whilst standing within that wash-room and smoking my very first cigarette, I never did wash my neck; this had finally proven to myself that I was being picked upon for no real reason. Being just a nipper in those days, it was not easy to confront the masters of yesteryear; I never had the nerve to do anything about the incident. Because of that one incident many years ago, I am still smoking today.

The Man on the Bike

When I was nine years old, Sunday was a day of peace and quiet. One would be very lucky to see a car upon the road. Sunday was a deserted day; one would also be a lucky person to see another person walking about the pavements, let alone a car upon the road. Sunday was the day of the Sabbath, a respected day by all; Sunday was like a ghost town; to see a cat, or even a dog, one had to be really lucky. There was no noise, no nothing. That one day a week seemed to be respected by all life itself. There was no playing in the streets, no shouting, crying, or hammering; there was not even the sound of birds; there was nothing.

But in saying that, there was one person who had the streets all to himself. In the early hours of Sunday mornings, and again upon the same Sunday evenings, there was a one-legged man riding upon a specially adapted push-bike; whilst riding his bike, he carried under one of his arms, a very long pole with a boat hook to one end. This man on the bike had one special strap fixed to the one peddle of his bike; this strap enabled him to peddle the bike by holding his good foot to the peddle under the strap. This one-legged man held tight to the very long pole under his left arm whilst steering the push-bike with his right hand; he carried the pole under his arm just like a knight in armour carrying his lance into battle. As a very young lad, every Sunday evening, I used to sit and wait upon a three feet high front garden wall, for this one-legged man to pass by; on occasions, when the man on the bike passed me by, I sensed that he was looking at me, as if I had a pair of horns fixed firmly to the top of my head. What this one-legged man was doing with this very long pole, that held a hook upon one end, was turning on and off the street lights. In those early years, this was the way it was done. The old iron lamppost in those days, that was changed over from gas to electric, was situated just off the kerbstone, upon the pavements adjacent to the gutter; unlike today, they are set further in upon the pavements away from the kerb. In the evenings, whilst still sat upon the bike, this one-legged man would on passing, and without stopping, place the hook end of the long pole into an eye upon a switch arm, that was set high at the top of the lamppost near to the bulb. The switch arm was an on off switch. After placing the hook end of the pole into the eye of the switch arm, he would then pull upon the pole with his left hand and arm to switch on the light; he would then unhook the pole without stopping his bike.

He and his bike were always on the move. When switching off the lights in the mornings, he would push the long pole, as opposed to pulling, to enable himself to switch off each single lamppost in turn.

This one-legged man never stopped peddling with his one leg as he had switched on or off all the street lights, that were situated all the way down one side of the road; he had it down to a fine art. After he had been all the way up one side of the road, he would then turn his bike around, then ride back down the opposite side of the road into my direction, to do the same thing all over again; on doing so, he would then for the second time, pass me by. I had waited every Sunday evening to see this one-legged man for one reason only; I was waiting for him to hook the eye upon the switch arm without stopping, and then to see him get himself caught up whilst still holding the long pole; hopefully, to see him pull himself completely off from his bike; but he never did. Fun in those days was what you made it, and I was very disappointed with this one-legged man; he had let me down; I was not a happy child.

The Schizophrenic Billy-Goat

In 1993 I reared a few goats upon a smallholding within the Salisbury area. There were times when some of the goats would get very boisterous and full of mischief whilst roaming about the grounds as I was repairing the barns. They were always underfoot and up to no good. There were also times when I would get a little annoyed, on catching one or two of the goats running off with a small bag of nails, or a packet of cigarettes, that I had placed down upon the grass next to where I was working. But at the end of the day, one can only but love them to death. One can never tell what they may get up to next; no two days were the same.

I had upon this smallholding ten goats in all. One of those goats was a very big mean and ill-tempered billy-goat; he was a schizophrenic. This big billy had put me upon my backside three times over the years. He was very fast, sly, and alert. I did not need a guard dog to protect the small-holding; he was more than a match for any person. Upon entering the smallholding by means of the main gate from the roadside, one had to look twice to see just where this big billy-goat was situated within the field; if one did not, then one would find out the hard way on entering into his domain unannounced that he was there. If this big billy-goat saw a person opening the main gate, this big mean old billy-goat would then wait for that person to enter and to be looking the other way before attacking his unexpected prey; this ill-tempered billy-goat would without warning butt that person so hard with its deadly curved horns, that hospital treatment would more than likely be required.

Having to let all the goats roam free around the fields was not always possible; there were times when I had to place them all in a holding pen; this was a twelve volt electric fence that most farmers would place around the perimeter of a field, to stop sheep getting out on to the road, or into other fields that belonged to another farmer. It is now necessary for myself to explain further at this point to those people who don't really know exactly what an electric fencing around a farmer's field consists of, for this electric fencing has a strong part to play within the remainder of my story. This fencing has a twelve volt battery laid upon the grass beside a post, with an earth wire from the battery then attached to the bottom strand of wire that runs all around the field upon metal stakes; the metal stakes are pushed into the soft soil approximately ten feet apart. The bottom strand of wire is set approximately two inches from the ground upon the metal stakes. A live lead running off from the same battery is then attached to a second strand of wire, that is again set at two inches apart above the first strand of wire. Another two strands of wire will then be added separately above each other as before. Having the electric fencing now set up and the power switched on, will in theory stop the sheep or goats going on through the fencing, or jumping over the top. The holding pen that I had erected did not go around the whole of the field, for I had placed the metal stakes four feet apart to one side of the field. Upon doing so, I had erected a ten square yard electric compound.

There were many reasons why I had erected this electric holding pen. One of the reasons was because I had to tether the billy-goat upon a chain within another part of the field, in order to give the nanny-goats a rest from him whilst they were in the mating season. Another reason for placing all the nannies in the holding pen was because the billy, when the nanny-goats were in season, reeked with a terrible disgusting sordid smell. If one were to touch the tethering chain that held the billy-goat in check, the smell upon one's hand would take a lot to remove; even when washed, it would take a full day for the smell that seeped into the pores of the skin to disappear. The billy-goat is the only one that emits the mating smell; the nannies are quite free of the mating smell, until the smell from the billy-goat rubs off on to them whilst mating. One could smell this billy-goat two hundred yards away; and boy, didn't he stink. When the mating season was over, the big billy-goat would then lose the disgusting odour that he had emitted from the sexual glands, and the air around him would then smell that much fresher. After the mating season was over, I would let the billy back off the chain to roam free; but on occasions, I would place him into the electric holding pen with the nannies. The reason now for placing the big billy-goat and the nanny-goats together in this holding pen, rather then letting them roam free as before, was simply to let the grass grow around them for another day, and at the same time, to keep the big billy-goat in check. If the big billy-goat had gotten free, he would find a way of getting out of the field through the hedges, or even the barb wire fencing that surrounds the smallholding, then on out into the road; upon escaping, the big old billy would take the nanny-goats with him. Once they had all escaped their place of safety; they would all deliberately tease me into catching them. If a person was on his own, it would take ages to round them all up.

Amongst the herd of nanny-goats and the big billy, was an eight month old billy; this little billy-goat was a replica of its father in every way. Upon one hot summer's day, I placed all the goats, including the schizophrenic big billy back into the electric holding pen. On the second day, the little eight month old billy-goat, had gotten himself from out of the electric holding pen. On seeing the young billy loose in the field, I picked him up, then gently placed him back over the twelve volt electrified wire of the holding pen. Unbeknownst to myself, the big schizophrenic billy-goat was watching my every move. After gently placing the little billy back into the holding pen, then walking away to approximately twelve feet in distance with my back now to all the goats, and the holding pen; I glanced back over my right shoulder to where I had left him; I was surprised to see that he was not there. Looking down behind myself, I could now see the young billy standing at the heels of my shoes looking up at me; picking up the young billy-goat once again, I then walked back to the holding pen to place him back in. After doing so, I walked away from the pen for the second time. On walking away, I again glanced back over my shoulder to where I had left him; again, he was right behind myself. Picking up the young offender once again, I walked back to the holding pen and dropped him to the ground as I reached over the top wire; on releasing the young billy, he immediately shot back through between the lower strands of wire out of the holding pen, as if the twelve volt voltage, were not there; on picking him up yet again, I decided to do something to him that even I did not like doing; but sometimes one has to be a little cruel to be kind. I did not want this young billy to find his way out and on to the road. Picking up the young billy, holding him tightly within my arms, I placed the tip of his nose upon the electric fencing wire; after the young goat had felt the voltage going through the wire upon his nose, I released him back into the holding pen; the young billy just stood within the pen looking back up at me, as if to say, 'That didn't hurt.' I was now adamant that the voltage that he felt through the wire upon his nose would now keep him in the pen. I again turned to walk away; as I did so, I again glanced back into the direction of the holding pen; the young billy-goat was not there; he was once again right behind myself. Again, I picked up the young goat and walked back to the holding pen. On reaching the holding pen, I stepped over the top wire to enter into the compound; on doing so, I tried to be a little bit more severe with this young goat for his future safety. Whilst standing inside the holding pen with the young billy still held within my arms, I placed his front lip upon the twelve volt wire; I was now hoping that this would register into its daft brain: that he must stay within the holding pen for his own safety. On letting him feel the current of the twelve volt electricity going through the wire and on to his lip, I had forgotten all about the big schizophrenic billy-goat, that was also somewhere inside the same holding pen. After I had given the young billy a taste of the wire fencing, I then said to the young goat as I placed him to the ground, 'Now maybe you will stay put; you will learn one way or the other, it was for your own safety.' I then stepped back and away from the fencing whilst still inside the holding pen. After gently putting the young billy down on to the ground, the young billy-goat looked back up at me as if he hadn't a care in the world. Looking at him, I would almost say that he had a smile about his loveable face as he had cheekily stood his ground; as I bent down again to pat him on the head, I was suddenly lifted two foot into the air, with an unexpected whack from the schizophrenic billy-goat; I came back down to earth only to be butted again straight into the live electric fencing; I then found myself entangled in the four-strand electric fencing like a wrestler, all tied up in the ropes of a boxing ring. I could feel the twelve volt charge of electricity running through all four strands of fencing wire into my own body, as both my arms and one leg was held fast in entanglement; I was not a happy person.

One of my sons, who had been watching all the while,

was rolling about the grass with laughter. From my tied position, I could see that the big schizophrenic billy-goat was springing up and down upon his back hind legs, just like the Lone Ranger's horse. The schizophrenic billy-goat was now getting ready to give to me another head-butt face on; I could see the big billy-goat's red fixed glazed eyes looking straight at me as he was about to give the third charge; momentarily, the readings that I was getting from his angry looks seemed to say, 'Take that! Now see if you like it.'

My son was filled with uncontrollable laughter as he was still rolling upon the grass in the field nearby. Before the schizophrenic billy-goat could make his third and final charge at me, I was able to free myself from my entanglement; very quickly, I jumped back over and out of the holding pen to safety, just as the big billy moved in with his deadly charge. I then looked to my son; there was no talking to him, he had tears in his eyes. I then turned to look at the goats within the holding pen; to my astonishment, all the goats were not within the holding pen. Momentarily, on looking at the electric wiring, I could see that two strands had been snapped apart; on my turn to look back into the holding pen from my son, the goats had walked unnoticed behind myself, and ran into the field. On turning back to see where they all had gotten to, I could see my son who had been laughing at me all the while being chased up the field by the big schizophrenic billy-goat, whilst all the other goats had set about grazing within the field. My son was now also not a happy person.

The Chicken Plucker

When I was about twenty years of age, I took a new job upon a farm in the Isle of Wight. The accommodation that was allocated to myself along with this new job was a tied cottage. A tied cottage was a rent-free dwelling that went with the farm job; if one was to end the contract of employment, then one would also have to give up the dwelling for the next person. The new job that I had undertaken, was that of an assistant to the chief herdsman, i.e. milking cows.

The chief herdsman was not much older then myself; he was a cruel sort of person and very mischievous. He was a master of the arts when it came to plucking a chicken.

Upon one bright and sunny day, I was walking down towards the milking shed; as I neared the milking shed, I could see that this chief herdsman was holding within his arms a beautiful red feathered cock bird. I asked the chief herdsman what was he going to do with this lovely looking bird; upon my asking, he looked at me with a grin, then laughed as he disappeared from view around the side of the milking shed; half an hour later, he re-emerged from behind the milking shed with the cock bird still held tightly within his hands, minus, its beautiful red feathers. The only feathers that I could see that were still left upon this cock bird were around the head, feet, and the very tips of both wings. This poor bird that was once proud and magnificent in all its finery, was now a very sorrowful looking specimen. The chief herdsman had somehow surgically removed all the beautiful red feathers without leaving any marks or visual harm to the cock bird.

The chief herdsman, upon his reappearance from behind the milking shed, smiled mischievously as I watched him release the cock bird back into a large chicken pen. Inside of this chicken pen, were approximately four dozen hen birds. The cock bird, who was now shamefully released without his beautiful red feathers, had made a mad dash on his release back into the pen. This once proud majestic looking bird, ran as fast as he could with a zigzagging motion, as he ran the gauntlet of the hen birds that were pecking at his naked body. The hens then chased him into the direction of the henhouse. Upon entering the henhouse, the featherless cock bird hid within one of the nesting boxes for three days and two nights. This once fine upright bird refused to emerge from the henhouse without his beautiful cloak of majestic looking feathers; on the fourth day, I found that the featherless cock bird had died from shame and embarrassment at the loss of his princely red coat that had reflected the sunlight in an array of wonderful colours.

The chief herdsman laughed hysterically at what he had just done, with tears falling from his eyes. I gave this once majestic looking bird an honourable burial; I put him in the pot. Two days later the chief herdsman was too ill to go to work. Tears were still falling from his eyes the next day; but not from laughter; he wasn't a happy person.

The Afterbirth

Upon that very same farm in the Isle of Wight some of the cows were due to give birth to young calves. The order of the day, was that the chief herdsman and I had to watch out for the afterbirth that sometimes dropped to the ground after a cow had given birth in the fields. The afterbirth from one of these cows, is enough to fill a full size dustbin. Most of the cows, if given the chance, would after giving birth to its young, eat the afterbirth. If a cow had eaten its own afterbirth, then there would be a very strong possibility of that cow choking to death; to make sure that this did not happen, one must remove the mass of afterbirth as soon as a calf is born. I for one, did not like the idea of doing that kind of work, for I must have the world's worst stomach; I had hopes of this never happening whilst I was employed upon the farm; but the inevitable had come to pass.

It was upon a very hot day, flies were out in force; they were everywhere. The chief herdsman and I were now out in open fields looking for the afterbirth amid the pregnant cows that wandered the fields. I was not a happy person. If we were to find a cow that had just given birth to a young calf, the afterbirth had to be picked back up from off the ground with a pitchfork; on picking it up with the pitchfork, it was like picking up spaghetti from off a dinner plate; one had to twist the handle around and around to enable oneself to pick it up in one lump; the thought of doing this made me feel quite ill. Looking at it heaped upon the ground was one thing, but to pick it back up was another.

The chief herdsman and I, had found such a cow after it had given birth. The chief herdsman, who knew about my very weak stomach, mischievously smiled as he proceeded to push the two-pronged pitchfork on into the slimy wet shining mass, that lay upon the ground; as I watched him winding the afterbirth up on to the pitchfork, I became violently sick. The chief herdsman continued to laughed at me, as he picked up the dripping afterbirth that hung loosely upon the end of his pitchfork. As he held the heavy mass aloft in my direction, the pitchfork started to bend under the weight; on seeing this dripping mass with countless swarms of flies, now engulfing the afterbirth that was glistening in the sunlight, I again continued to be violently sick with never-ending flows of tears streaming down both sides of my cheeks.

Seeing my predicament, the chief herdsman decided to take advantage of my dilemma; I was not a happy person. Full of outright wickedness, he chased me across the fields with the wet dripping mass outstretched upon his pitchfork before himself; I was running for dear life. Sick and heaving as I ran, I could just see between the sick tears that cob-webbed my eyes, his sickly grin that was as slimy as the afterbirth; the flies had also decided to join into the chase above his stupid head.

But alas, fate had called in his last card. As he was chasing me across the fields, he slipped upon a piece of wet slimy afterbirth that had dripped from the pitchfork ahead of himself. The bulk mass of slimy afterbirth, that hung momentarily above his stupid head upon the pitchfork, fell from off the pitchfork, down upon himself; the whole mass of shiny wet glistening slime, totally swamped him from head to foot as it fell off from the pitchfork on to his back; there was not very much of the chief herdsman's body to be seen from under the slithering slimy afterbirth, that blanketed his person; I stood and watched him for a moment or two, by peering between my fingers that partially covered my eyes, as he squirmed under the slimy mass that had spread across his own person whilst lying face down upon the ground. He himself was now not a happy person. The mass of afterbirth looked like a giant jellyfish covering its prey as it wobbled like jelly on top of him. As he tried to throw off the slimy afterbirth, I could see that he too was now being sick. I myself, was ill for two days after that little incident; my future upon that farm did not look too bright. In fact, it was short-lived.

The Stampede

Once again, upon that very same farm, it was milking time. Twice a day the chief herdsman and I would walk up to the top fields to where the cows were grazing; on reaching the top fields, we had to round up the cows into one herd, then drive them all back down to the milking sheds. Normally, the cows would come on down from the top fields to the gate on their own, upon recognising the voice command or whistle. Upon this particular hot sunny day, the chief herdsman and I decided to walk up the field to meet the cows, which were already walking back down towards us from the fields. Upon meeting the cows half-way up the field, we both turned to walk back down with the cows now following close to our heels. Whilst walking slowly back, I said to the chief herdsman, 'I bet that I can make these cows stampede.'

He replied, 'Rubbish! You have been watching too many films; you will never make them stampede; no way!'

After he had given me his view upon a stampede, I slowly dropped back to the rear of the herd; once I had gotten myself into position to the rear of all the cows, I then shouted insanely, and flapped my arms about whilst jumping up and down. The chief herdsman, who was still walking slowly, lazily down the field ahead of the herd, with both his hands set deep into the pockets, turned his head on hearing my shouting and a thunder of hoofs; on seeing the stampeding herd almost on top of himself, he ran like crazy; frantically, the chief herdsman tried to get out of their way by jumping into a hedgerow for safety. Upon his own reappearance from within the hedgerow, he was covered from head to foot in stinging nettles. He sure wasn't a happy person that day.

The Hedge Cutter

Many years ago, a lot of farmers used to have their own odd-job man working about the farms; they were traditionally known then as the hedge cutters. The hedge cutters' main job was that of cutting hedgerows, and the clearing out of all the rubbish and weeds that had accumulated within the ditches that were situated upon the country roads, around the outside perimeters of the farms. In those good old days, the hedge cutter cut the hedges with a pair of hand shears, unlike today, when they now use a modern machine.

One particular male hedge cutter who springs to mind when I myself was working upon a farm in the Isle of Wight, was living in a tied cottage that had been built back to back. My neighbour, the hedge cutter, was about sixty years old, very fat, and never ever had a change of clothing; he was slightly slow of mind, and very, very cantankerous; he also smelled something terrible.

Once a week, he would set off upon foot down the old country roads to the local village dole office; at the local dole office, the hedge cutter would ask them if they had found him a wife yet. This went on for months. Finally, he had gotten fed up with the waiting. Out of desperation, the hedge cutter approached my wife upon a country road, as she was on her way back from the village shop; he asked my wife if she would leave me for him, and then move back into his own dirty cottage with him. He then told her that he would pay her handsomely for favours received. My wife, who was then very young, had immediately pushed him into a water-filled ditch, which he himself was getting ready to clean out of all the weeds and overgrowth. I believe that was the only bath that he had in years. He wasn't a happy person.

The Hole in the Ground

That very same hedge cutter was looking over a farm hedge upon one bright sunny day; on the other side of the hedgerow was a very quiet country road; upon that road were two local council workmen, who had dug a very big hole quite near to the ditch beside the hedge; whilst the two workmen were making this hole a little deeper, the old cantankerous hedge cutter, after peering over the top of a privet hedge, found his way through a gap in the boundary hedgerow; the hedge cutter, who was now standing upon the country road watching what the two workmen were doing, started up a conversation between them; it did not take too long for an argument to arise between the three. The hedge cutter, who had only been there for approximately two minutes, tried to tell the workmen how they should dig the hole; one of the workmen then told the old hedge cutter to clear off, and to attend to his own business; this old hedge cutter got very stubborn and even more cantankerous over the whole affair relating to the digging of the hole; he refused to move away, until they had both listened to what he considered to be the right and proper way to dig the hole.

After five minutes had gone by, one of the workmen started to clamber back up out of the hole which was now already approximately five feet deep, by four feet square. The workman, on climbing back out from the hole, was now in a terrible rage. On his way out from the hole, he picked up a shovel; the workman, who was now very annoyed and very upset over the old hedge cutter telling him on how to dig a hole, smacked the old hedge cutter over the head with the shovel. The old hedge cutter, who now had a rather sore head, was off work for two days after that little caper; the smack on the head with the shovel from the workman hadn't changed him one bit; in fact, I think it had made him even more cantankerous. He definitely wasn't a happy person.

The Rain

When I worked upon a farm in the Isle of Wight, I saw an amazing unexpected phenomenal sight that was for myself, something that I will always treasure.

Upon one very hot and sunny day, I was looking up and across at the clear blue sky; I could see in the far distance, heavy rain clouds slowly coming in from across the sea. The thunder and lightning was sounding very loud as the heavy rain clouds slowly drifted across the sky towards myself; ten minutes later, something extraordinary happened. I was walking upon a pavement near to the sea front in Freshwater Bay, upon this glorious and very hot Indian summer's day, when suddenly, down from out of the sky, came this downpour of very large hailstones; and yet, I was still dry as a bone standing in the very hot sun. The downpour of hailstones was right in front of myself and bouncing off the pavement, it was unbelievable; it was as if I were standing in front of a very thick sheet of glass. Standing there, with one hand now outstretched into this wall of hailstones was unnatural; it was also unbelievable to see the hailstones bouncing at the toes of my dry shoes to the front of myself, whilst hitting the ground with tremendous force; there were hailstones in their millions running in a straight line to the left and the right of myself; the hailstones were almost the size of small marbles; I had never seen such big ones. Seeing them, gave to me the strangest feeling to have witnessed such an event.

Everyone knows, that the rain must end, and begin

somewhere, but this beats the lot. Depending on where you are situated at the time, one will find that the rain usually just frizzles out upon the edges of a heavy downpour; the same being with hailstones. Sometimes, the end or the beginning of rain storms just turns to a slight mist or a very fine spray. Some people say that the change to the weather condition over the Isle of Wight has something to do with the needles, I personally do not know why; but it was a very strange experience.

For the second time in that same week, I again witnessed a very similar strange phenomenon; my second sighting, of an uncanny similar situation, that I considered myself lucky to have been a part of at that time, was while I sat upon the upper deck of a double-decker bus; it was again a very hot and sunny day. Upon looking out from the window of the bus to the right of myself, I could see that the rain was absolutely pouring down; and yet, looking out of the window to the left of myself; it was a dry sunny hot day. Other people have also told me that they too have witnessed the very same strange phenomena. Both of those strange and amazing unexpected phenomenal sightings that I myself have witnessed will now also be an experience within another chapter of my life that I will never forget.

The Shock

Some years ago, whilst I was working upon a farm in Freshwater Bay on the Isle of Wight, something unexpectedly happened to the farmhouse that I was living in. But before I tell you what happened to my little old farmhouse, I must tell you a short story that leads to my finding out, that my house was now not what it should be. I was at the time, milking the cows to one end of the milking shed, whilst the chief herdsman was working down the far end. There were approximately ten cows in a row being milked by machines. The milking machines known as clusters, were in those days very much up to date; just as I was milking the very last cow at the end of the row, I could hear this laughing coming from the other end of the milking shed; the laughter could only belong to one other person, the chief herdsman. Leaving the work that I was doing, I went to see what he was laughing about. At the other end of the milking shed I found the chief herdsman sitting upon a stool, treating a cow for mastitis, whilst chuckling to himself. Upon my asking him what was so funny, he looked up and said as he continued the treatment on the cow's udders, 'Your house has fallen down!' I then told him that there was more crap coming out of him than out of all the cows' arses. The chief herdsman, continued to chuckle quietly to himself as I turned to walk back to the other end of the milking shed. On resuming my work, I could again hear him laughing to himself. Getting a little pissed off with him, I again left my place of work to see what he kept laughing about. Upon confrontation, I asked, 'Now what!'

He again repeated in a very quiet voice, 'Your house has fallen down.'

Standing there for a moment or two, looking down on him tending to a sick cow, and chuckling to himself, I decided to go and have a look for myself. One could never take the chief herdsman seriously, for he was a great joker; but there were times when he was not clowning; the trouble with him, was that one could not tell a lie from the truth.

On my arrival at the house, I found that he was telling the truth. What I had found was that the prevailing winds had loosened the apex to the front of the cottage, thus causing the heavy brickwork upon the front apex to collapse. The falling brickwork had embedded itself deep into the soil outside near to the front door. On entering the cottage, I found my stressed-out wife crying hysterically and shaking profusely. That was the final straw; I now had had enough of farm life. My wife and I weren't happy persons. Following that incident, I gave in my notice; two days later, my wife and I returned to Southampton, our home town. Both my wife and I never set foot upon the Isle of Wight again.

The Radio

Whilst working as a binman in the dark winter months upon the City of Southampton's corporation dust carts, a very strange occurrence gave me a mind-boggling almost unexplained incident; on getting up for work early one morning, I came down from the upstairs bedroom, then on into the downstairs front room to where I kept an old valve radio. These old valve radios, when they were first switched on, took a little time to warm up before they would start to work. After switching on the old radio, I walked from the front room, down a passageway, then into the kitchen; whilst I was placing the kettle on the gas stove, I heard a strange sound coming from the front room. Thinking that it must be my stressed-out wife getting up and coming down the stairs, I shouted out, 'What's the time?' Then the strangest thing happened. A man's deep voice boomed back at me from the other end of the passage, just as I was about to pick up the teapot, 'It's seven o'clock!' I wasn't a happy person.

Upon hearing this strange man's voice, I instinctively ran into the passageway looking for the intruder, who was without a doubt somewhere within my home. I could not see the intruder in the passageway as I made my way towards the front room; on entering the front room, the outside street light that was adjacent to the window, had dimly lit the room from between the slightly open curtains. I scanned the dimly lit shadowy room, with piercing eyes from the entrance into the front room, to where I had stopped; he was not there either. Then it dawned upon me; the radio. A thought had come to mind, just as the radio started to play music. What had truly happened, was that the radio had just finished warming up at that point in time, thus, the man's deep voice answered my question. Between hearing the man's voice, and myself running into the front room from the passageway to look for an intruder, the radio had paused between the speaking and the music. On my realisation of the truth, I did feel an idiot.

The Breakdown

On the Friday of 23rd August, 1996, my van had broken down upon the Salisbury – Stockbridge Road; the fan belt upon my classic J4 van had broken. My son, who was in the AA, walked a half mile to a farmhouse to find a phone; the AA said that they would get to us as soon as they could. After my son and I had waited half an hour, a contract mobile mechanic on hire to the AA arrived in a transit breakdown truck with all its lights flashing. The mechanic was a welcome sight. On getting out from the breakdown vehicle, the mechanic, who was getting on in years, asked me what was wrong with the van. After I told the mechanic that it was a broken fan belt, the mechanic searched amongst his stock within the breakdown vehicle to see if he could accommodate me with the much needed part; as luck would have it, he found a replacement fan belt. The mechanic then told me that he was sixty-three years of age, and was due to retire; he was wearing upon his hands a pair of leather gloves; this I thought to be a little strange, as it was now summer. The mechanic set about replacing the fan belt from inside the cab on my J4 van. After ten minutes had passed by, the mechanic had got back down from my van for a rest. The mechanic looked to me and remarked, 'I can't undo the nuts on the alternator, it's my hands, I have crumbling bone disease, I can't grip anything properly.'

'Can anything be done about your hands?' I asked with concern.

'If I were to have an operation, I won't be able to move

either of my wrists; it's a fifty-fifty chance on whether the operation will be successful or not; so I'm not going to bother about having the operation.'

I then looked to this old chap and said, 'Here, let me do it, you have another rest.'

Five minutes later, I had replaced the fan belt back on to my J4 van. The old gent then said, 'I will not charge you for the fan belt, seeing you have done all the work.'

I looked at the poor old chap and replied, 'All right mate, that's fine.' He was a happy mechanic.

The mechanic then got back into his breakdown truck. Upon driving off, he had given to my son and I a feeble wave. My son and I could not believe that the AA would send out a person with his condition to repair vehicles. But that's exactly what they did do. I did feel sorry for the old chap.

The Clock

Some years ago, I had gone to bed at six in the evening, as I had to leave for work at twelve midnight, to deliver four drums of diesel to three tractors which were working a night contract. I told my stressed-out wife to set the alarm clock for twelve o'clock that night. Upon waking up, I found my wife to be asleep and I was late for work; the clock did not sound the alarm. I was fuming and I shouted at my stressed-out wife, and ordered her to get a new clock for the coming of that day. On that following day in the evening upon my return to my home from work, my stressed-out wife was pleased to inform me that she had bought the new alarm clock with a double bell. That very night, my wife set the alarm clock for three thirty in the morning, this being a new time to start work for that following day. Bedtime was soon upon us; after a hard day's work, we both went to bed at eleven o'clock; it wasn't long before we had both fallen into a deep sleep.

The alarm clock started to ring, it was time to get up. On turning off the noise of the clock, I sleepily clambered out of the bed over my wife to wash and dress; after dressing by the light of the moon shining on through the window, I sat down to have a cup of tea in the dark, so as not to wake my stressed-out wife. Ten minutes later, my stressed-out wife was awoken upon hearing me muttering to myself; 'What's the matter now?' she shouted in a sleepy voice.

'Why do I feel so tired?' I asked miserably whilst sitting

in the dark.

'I don't know!' she shouted angrily.

'What's the time?' I shouted back, as she buried her head deep in under the bed coverings.

'What's the time?' I asked again whilst yawning and stretching my neck.

'I told you! I don't know! Have a look at the clock!' she shouted back from under the bed coverings. On switching the light on, I fumbled for my glasses to have a look at the clock; finding my glasses, I tried to look to the new clock amid the bright light from the light bulb that was now hurting my eyes. Shielding my eyes from the light, and then trying to focus my red eyes on to the face of the clock, I could not believe in what I was now looking at; the new clock portrayed the time at twelve o'clock! Going by that clock, I only had an hour's sleep. I could not understand why the alarm had gone off. I then looked to the old clock; I found that the alarm upon the old clock that did not go off the night before, was the one that had awoken me. Now I know why I was still feeling so tired. Picking up the old clock, I flung it out of the window in temper. Taking my clothing back off, I entered back into the bed next to my stressed-out wife for a good night's sleep. Morning was soon upon me, I was again late for work. I wasn't a happy person.

The Light

A few years ago, when I was living in the Sholing area of Southampton, there was a power cut. Living opposite me were two old ladies who always sat within their front window looking out, whilst taking it in turns to style each other's hair. The two old ladies' curtains were open day and night. One of the old ladies would sit in a chair, whilst the other ran a comb through the grey mass of hair upon her friend's head. They would both do the same old thing, day in, and day out. I'm surprised that they haven't made each other bald over the years for the amount of combing that they do to each other. What they were really doing, was being downright nosy. They would both watch every person who passed their window. Not one person within the street would escape their nosiness. Most of the time, they would both be looking over to my home directly opposite, to see if they could see what was going on through my own front window; they would both look on through my window from their own, to see if they could see something or anything that was worth talking about.

Upon one dark winter's night, there was a power cut; to compensate for the loss of the electric light, I ran a twelve volt running lead from a car battery, up the wall, and along the ceiling to hang down alongside the original light bulb; on the end of the lead, I attached a car headlight bulb. The light from the car bulb brightly lit up my living-room. Having my curtains still wide open, the light from the car bulb shone on out through my window to mix with the very dark moonless night. Looking out from my window into the dark outside, I could just see up and down to the opposite side of the road. Whilst I was looking out of the window, I could see that only two of the houses out of twenty had candles that were flickering dimly in their windows; the candles threw out an illuminating shadowy light on to the road, whilst all the other houses were in total darkness, including the nosy old ladies across the way. I could barely see the local telephone box on the corner that was also without light; one could only just see the silhouette of the telephone box amid the dark of the night. One hour later after putting up my makeshift light, there was a knock upon my front door. On opening the door, I could see standing there before me one of the old ladies from across the road. 'Excuse me! Can you please tell me why it is that you have got your house light on, whilst all the rest of us in the street have none?' she asked feebly, with a nosy look about her person.

'Yes!' I answered with a smirk. 'As you know, I work for the local council upon the dust carts; because I work for the local council, they have quite simply left my light on; it's the perks of the job I'm afraid madam,' I added with a straight face.

That's not fair!' shouted the old woman; 'I'm going to give them a mouthful over this! What gives you the right to be over us? We're only old age pensioners, we should have free lighting; it's not right!' she shouted with a jealous spiteful voice.

'Well, that's the way it is,' I replied as she turned to storm across the darkened road. She wasn't a happy person.

After shutting the front door behind her, I went back to the front room window; at the window, I looked out to see where she had gone to; not surprisingly, she was heading straight down the road to the unlit phone box on the corner; after making her call, presumably to the local council offices, and the electricity board, she then hobbled back from the street corner telephone box, to her own home opposite. Her friend, who was still peering out from the window into the dark of the night, was waiting patiently for her return.

The next day, they both were once again sat within their window looking out as usual, doing each other's hair. The looks that they both gave me were of stone.

The Commanding Officer

Years ago, when I was in the Territorial Army, we used to go away for the weekends to the gun ranges for target practice; upon my return home on a late Sunday evening, I was dropped off at my home by my fellow comrades in an army truck; there were in all, three army trucks and one champ. In the back of these army trucks, were fellow uniformed part-time soldiers, who were all fully armed with 303s. In the lead of those trucks, was the army champ; this being a vehicle that looked like a cross between a jeep and a Land Rover; sitting inside the champ were three commanding officers and a driver. Upon getting out from the rear end of a army truck, the commanding officers saluted me as I stood upon the pavement near to my home before pulling off. When they had gone, I sat down within my home having a cup of tea. Ten minutes later, there was a knock upon the front door. On opening the front door, I could see standing there one of my fully uniformed comrades; he informed me that the army champ and the trucks were back outside, and that a commanding officer wanted to see me. Following closely behind my soldier in arms back to the pavement outside, we stopped by the army champ that was parked to the kerb; 'Yes sir!' I said with a salute whilst still in uniform.

The commanding officer then said, 'We have just driven around the block, and then remembered that you had not signed the forms for the six weeks' training away with the unit in August. Will you please sign these papers now, to say that it is all right for yourself to go.' After the commanding officer passed to me a pen and the forms to sign, I placed my signature upon the required forms, then handed them back to him on a return salute. All the other officers who were sat within the army champ, saluted me upon driving off. The next day, the two nosy old ladies from across the street asked my wife, 'What was the army doing outside of your home yesterday?' My wife told them that they had come back for their orders, giving to the nosy old ladies the impression that I was an army high commanding officer, and not of a common private in the TA. That following day, I walked down to the local shop; on my entry into the shop, I was greeted by an unusual, 'Yes sir, no sir,' by the shopkeeper and other shoppers who lived in the same road as myself. Looking around the shop slightly bewildered, I could see the two old ladies who lived opposite myself, standing in one corner of the shop whispering. On seeing them, I then remembered my wife telling me what she had said to the nosy old ladies the day before. On remembering, I gave to them both in turn, a smile, followed by a slight gentlemanly bow, as an officer and a gentleman would do; they both then smiled back at me with a returned slight bowing movement. They both looked to be quite proud, to be living opposite a high commanding officer. We never did tell the nosy old trouts the truth. They were a happy pair of old fogies.

The Army Shirt

At the tender age of eighteen, I joined the Territorial Army as a drummer bugler. The army clothing in those days was of the flannel type, and felt a little rough against the skin. The army shirt, this being the main issue within this story, was very long, and looked more like a dress when worn without any other clothing. Its length was well past the knees.

When I was in the Territorial Army, we all used to go away on the weekends, to other ranges in different counties; upon one of those weekends away, we were stationed near a town, not too far from the New Forest. Being allowed to leave the billets in the evenings, myself and two comrades went to town in full uniform, to visit the many different pubs. After having a few drinks, I went into the toilets of a pub to do the number two! Upon breaking my neck to get to the toilets before it was too late, I started to undress myself as I entered into the toilets; I had just enough time to take off my webbing belt, then to drop my heavy flannelled trousers down to my ankles before sitting myself down on to the toilet pan. Sitting there with a sigh of relief upon the throne, after yesterday's dinner had made its exit down and into the pan, I began to think about the next day's training. As I sat there deep in thought, something suddenly struck me. I then said to myself, 'Wait a minute! I did not hear yesterday's dinner go down the pan?' Looking back down between my legs into the pan under the top flap of my shirt, that covered the tops of my knees, I then said to myself, 'Oh no!' What had happened to the number two was now quite clear; the dress type shirt that I was wearing, was still situated around the back of my legs, as I had sat myself down upon the throne; yesterday's dinner was now trapped within the seat of my shirt as if it were a hammock. Taking out my Swiss Army Knife, I had to cut the army shirt down from the waist past the knees, then to make a second cut around my waist in order to get away from my predicament. I wasn't a happy person. Ever since that day, I cut all my army shirts short; just in case I had another emergency.

The Bucket

When I was twelve years old, my mother, who in many ways resembled Old Mother Reilly, had an argument with my father; my father was moaning about the stairs not being very clean; he was always moaning about something or nothing. One day, my mother, who was not happy about my father keeping on about the state of the stairs, waved her arms about, and then rolled up her sleeves as she said, 'Right you bastard! I'll give you clean the stairs, you wait and see; you will never ask me to do them again.' What Mother had done, was to highly polish the lino that ran the length of a very steep wooden stair, from top to bottom; the next morning, I was ordered by my father, as it was my turn out of ten, to go around all the bedrooms to empty all the piss buckets. The easiest way to do this, was to tip all the urine out of all the buckets into one. The bucket that I was filling was, like the others, galvanised. In those days, this heavy bucket did not make the job any lighter; when the galvanised bucket was filled, I had to carry it on down the stairs, then on through the house, to the outside toilet.

Upon this day of the argument between my mother and father, I had emptied all the buckets into one as usual; after filling the bucket to almost overflowing from the other buckets that were situated within the upstairs bedrooms, I made my way to the top of the stairs. Upon reaching the top of the stairs, I was wearing an oversize pair of socks, that had been handed down to me from one of my older brothers; I was about to slowly descend the stairs with this full bucket of urine, when suddenly as the heels of my oversized socks connected with the newly highly polished lino upon the second step down from the top, I slipped, the bucket went up in the air with its full contents raining back down upon my head; momentarily, I slid from top to bottom upon the wet lino, with the bucket and a torrent of urine cascading down behind myself. I was soaked right through to the bones. As I reached the bottom of the stairs upon my back, feet first, the bucket hit me on the back of my head with a smack as I was about to get back up; I was that dizzy, I felt as if I were pissed out of my head. I was not a happy person.

The Lamppost

When I was seventeen I was a little fed up and really pissed off; because I was fed up and pissed off, I had decided to go for a walk. My walk took me down a road called Augustine Road in Northam Road, Southampton; this being just around the corner from where I lived. As I was walking along this road upon the kerb edge of the pavement, with both my hands in my pockets, I was deep in thought. The day was very hot and sunny. Slowly I continued on with my snail-paced walk along the kerb edge of the pavement with my head lowered. Suddenly, just as I looked up, I hit my head with a severe blow upon a cast-iron lamppost.

Holding my head with both hands to relieve the pain, I continued to walk further along the road upon the kerb edge of the pavement; as I did so, I peered between my fingers as I was holding my head to see who was watching me. I sensed that there were people looking at me from behind the curtains of the nearby homes. I felt such a fool walking into a lamppost, I was hoping that no one had noticed my little accident. Feeling very embarrassed, I looked back over my shoulder at the lamppost whilst holding my head with one hand; as I turned to face in the direction that I was walking, I immediately and unexpectedly hit my head upon a second lamppost. The pain inflicted upon the same lump to my head was unbearable. I was definitely not a happy person. I never felt so stupid and doubly embarrassed in my life.

My snail-pace walk along the kerb of the pavement had

come to a halt, as I stood there looking at the second lamppost, whilst holding my bruised head with two hands; on easing the double impact upon my now very sore head with two hands, I once again looked about myself, to see if I was being watched. The road looked deserted, as I also scanned the front windows of the nearby houses. I had this overpowering feeling, that there were people out there somewhere watching my every move.

Unbeknownst to myself, the local council had erected a second cast iron lamppost, that fell short of the normal distance between each lamppost allowed; the new lamppost, as I found out later, was erected to help the old-age people, who were coming out from the church hall in the late evenings. Nightly functions on Bingo were held frequently within the church hall for the old-aged; without this second street light, the entrance out from the church hall for the old people, would have been very dark and dangerous for them; unlike myself, now having two very dark eyes; I have since seen the error of my ways, and have never, never, walked upon the kerb of a pavement again.

The Rowing Boat

When I was fourteen, my old dad, who was a bit of a scoundrel, had a small flat-bottom rowing boat. He kept this flat-bottom rowing boat in the back garden to the rear of the house. The house that we lived in was situated in Radcliffe Road, Northam, Southampton.

This flat-bottom boat that was given to my old dad had a very large hole to its underside; my old dad, being a clever sort of chap, set about the repairing of the hole with great expectations. The boat being made of wood, the repair should have been a simple task. My old dad repaired this boat, by lining the inside, bottom and sides with heavy tin, and then using two-inch nails to hold the tin in place; after patching half the boat with tin, he then covered the whole inside, bottom and the sides with road tar; the road tar, had been melted down upon the gas stove in my mother's kitchen whilst using her galvanised bucket; my mother was not a happy person. The inside bottom of the boat, had an inch-thick layer of tar that ran the whole length of the boat. My old dad applied the hot wet tar to the inside bottom of the boat by using my mother's long-handled sweeping brush. My dear old mum was once again not a happy person. When the tar had dried, my relations helped my dear old dad and my brothers to turn the boat upside down. Having the boat now upside down made it easier for my old dad to tar the outside bottom.

A week later, when the tar had fully dried, my old dad decided that this flat-bottom boat, was now ready for the open sea. It then took ten of us, all brothers and cousins, to move the boat from out of the rear garden, on through the house, and then out on to the pavement. The boat was very heavy; the strain upon all ten lifting this flat-bottom boat to its new position was immense. Now having the boat to the front of the house upon the pavement, all ten lifted the boat once again upside down. Having the boat now upside down, we all then lifted the boat gently upon a large pram; my dear old mum was not amused. Having the boat now upon the pram created an argument between my old dad and my dear old mum; we all struggled to push the pram half a mile to the end of the road; but, one third of the way down the road, the pram collapsed under the weight of the boat. The pram's wheels had twisted and buckled under the strain; they were beyond repair. We now had no choice but to leave the broken pram upon the pavement. I looked upon the face of my old dad, and knew what he was thinking as he stood looking at the now discarded pram; I could see upon my old dad's face whilst he stood chewing upon the stem of his pipe to one side of his mouth, that he was in deep, deep shit with my dear old mum. My dear old mum would definitely be doing her own tarring and feathering upon my old dad's return back home.

Having lost our only transport that was to take the boat to the end of the road, we all set about pulling the boat with the use of ropes. All ten, with ropes now laid across each of their shoulders in line behind each other, like Egyptian slaves pulling blocks of stone to the pyramids, we all started to drag the flat-bottom boat onwards. It was quite a sight to the people living within the road to see ten men, one behind the other, pulling and dragging this heavy boat along the road; there were people from nearby houses watching the parading spectacle upon this boat's incredible journey to its launching place. Neighbouring people within the road were also looking out of their windows, waving and whistling. There were many more of the same standing upon the pavements and in the kerbsides as we journeyed onwards. The people in the street were all watching, as if it were some sort of carnival as the heavy boat noisily passed them by. The heavily tarred boat was scraping its bottom upon the road surface; in its wake, fresh tar marks, and scraping marks from the underside of the boat had left their calling card. The boat was dragged upon its underside until we had reached the end of the road. At the end of the road, we had to enter through two big opened gates; this being the entrance to the old Block Crete, where they had made the old breeze blocks for the many different building trades, that were situated in and around Southampton. Passing now on through the gates, we dragged the boat further onwards, until we had breathtakingly stopped at the embankment's edge. The embankment's edge was the end of our journey to the River Itchen. Looking down from the embankment's edge, that was handmade from large flagstones sloping very steeply on down into the water; we could see that it was not going to be an easy task to launch the boat. Before putting the boat into the water, we all decided to christen the boat *Titanic*!

After we had named the vessel, all ten pushed the heavy flat-bottom boat to the very edge of the embankment. The *Titanic* was now balancing upon the very edge of the embankment like a see-saw; with its bow overhanging the slope, we all paused for a moment to assess our possibilities. We were all now leaning on the rear end of the boat discussing our present position for the safety of the craft. After agreeing upon a solution, we all eased our body weights from off the rear end of the *Titanic*. Together, with the use of body power, and a little bit more sweat, we lifted the rear end of the boat up, until the front bow was tilted into the downward position. Having the *Titanic* now resting its whole underside upon the sloping flagstones, and facing downwards into the direction of the water's edge, everyone was getting themselves into position, to help the *Titanic* upon its maiden voyage. All hands were now to the rear of the boat; with one hefty push, the heavy flat-bottom boat started to slide under its own weight down the embankment. As the *Titanic* took its final journey on down the embankment and picked up speed, we all gave a victorious cheer.

Our loud cheers suddenly stopped as we all watched the *Titanic* hit the water's edge nose on; the *Titanic* immediately disappeared at speed, to the bottom of the sea and out of sight; there was silence, as we all stood there looking at each other, then back to the remaining bubbles upon the surface of the water to where the *Titanic* was last seen. Not another word was spoken as we all stood with dismay upon all our faces. After all our efforts; the busted pram, the launch of the *Titanic*; all gone; it was now a sad day. After a moment or two had passed in total silence, we all looked upon each other as if in mourning; then fell about laughing. My old dad just stood there with a glum face, as he once again chewed upon the stem of his pipe. He stood sorrowfully looking back down into the watery grave at the last remaining bubbles, where the *Titanic* had met its final fate; he too roared with laughter, as he recognised the funny side of our efforts and misfortune. My old dad never did repair another boat after that. At least he had the right name for the boat.

The Chicken

In the good old days, my dear old dad was the only one allowed to cut up the Sunday roast. More often then not, the roast joint upon the Sunday table each week turned out to be a chicken that my old dad had poached from a nearby farm. Eight of us would all sit around a very large wooden table watching, and waiting, for our dear old dad to cut the Sunday roast into equal shares. On watching our dear old dad cutting up the meat, we would all sit around the wooden table and watch his every move as he passed each separate piece of meat in turn upon a fork around the table and on to the plates. My old dad, who was the supreme master and overlord of the house, always sat at the head of the table. Whilst the overlord was handing out the equal shares of the meat about the table, my dear old mum would sit back and away from the table, to await the ending of our meals, before she herself could sit down and have hers.

Every Sunday was the same, we would all sit and watch our dear old dad in total silence as he cut wafer thin the tasty looking golden brown roast joint, or chicken, with his very sharp ex-army sheaf knife, and then scrape it from off the fork with the aid of his knife on to the plates, as he went around the table clockwise. Whilst our dear old dad was dishing out the meat, we all would sit watching each other's plates with jealous and hungry eyes, to see who might have gotten, unexpectedly, a slightly bigger piece than the others. After our dear old dad had finished placing a small amount of wafer thin meat upon all our plates, it then left only his own plate to load up. We all sat very patiently and quietly with our hands upon our own laps under the wooden table, as we watched our dear old dad cut himself off a huge lump of meat, then to manoeuvre the lump of golden brown meat back on to his own extra large plate from the roasting pan with a fork. As we all sat there, we all looked back down at our own plates, then to each other's; and then once again, back to his.

After dear old dad had placed the remaining left-over meat from the roasting pan on to a plate, our dear old mum would pick up the remaining meat to take back out into the scullery to where the meat safe was situated. Having placed the remainder of the chicken or beef back into the meat safe, the meat safe was then locked with a very large padlock. My old dad would then go around the table with the roast potatoes as he had done with the meat. After gingerly placing the smallest roast potatoes on to each plate in turn, he would then place the biggest roast potatoes upon his own plate. When dear old dad had finished giving out an equal share to each member of the family, we would all look down at each other's plate simultaneously as before, then back to our own plates. After noting the size of each other's dinner, all eyes would then once again look back to our dear old dad's. Finally, when the dishing out of the dinners was completed, we would all then look to see where our share of the meat was hiding beneath the gravy. On picking up a soup spoon each, we all would then start to tuck into the meals before us. To make my own meal last longer, I would sit and read the newspaper table-cloth, as I slowly spooned away at the Sunday dinner. The leftovers, if any, were then given to the dog who had made a permanent home under the table about our feet. After everything was cleared away, two of my brothers and I would then go apple scrumping to fill the remaining spaces that were left within our partly full stomachs. Every Sunday evening, the left-over meat that was put back into the meat safe by our dear old mum, would become sandwiches for the master of the house, whilst the rest of us had bread and jam before going to bed.

Upon one late and very hot evening in the summer months of August, I became very brave towards the head of the family. My act of bravery happened upon my and my brother's return home from the local theatre; I was absolutely starving. Whilst sitting with my brother in the kitchen beside an empty table, reading the new table-cloth, I began to think about the chicken that was left over from Sunday. Looking into the dimly lit scullery that had no light of its own through an open adjoining door, I could just see within the shadows of the darkened scullery, the meat safe. With a wide smile, I said to my brother, 'I'm going to have a look into the meat safe!'

My brother replied, 'Don't! Dad is only sat in the other room watching the television with Mum, he will know that you have been at it!'

I then replied, 'Sod him; I'm starving.'

Standing up from the chair, I then stepped out from the well-lit kitchen, into the unlit dark shadowy scullery. Upon stepping out, and down one single small wooden step into the scullery from the kitchen, the light from the kitchen was blocked by my own person, I had to feel my way past the cooker to reach the meat safe. On reaching the meat safe, I found the lock was left open. Quietly opening the door on the meat safe, I could see the silhouette of a half-used chicken upon a plate. Grabbing the chicken from off the plate with one hand, I then placed two hands upon the chicken, as it neared my mouth like a hungry caveman. Whilst still facing the dark shadowy meat safe, I savagely took a very large mouthful from off the soft slushy tasting mouth-watering chicken carcass, with one huge bite, and then swallowed it on down in one satisfying gulp. As the tasty chicken slid on down the back of my throat, I had the most glorious feeling of contentment and satisfaction as it then entered my stomach. On my turning a full circle to face the kitchen entrance, that emitted a dim light, my brother simultaneously shut the kitchen door so that my old dad would not catch me at it. I was now standing in total darkness. As I blindly felt my way forward, a small flicker of light from the moon had emitted itself through the scullery window, subsequently helping me see my way forward towards the unseen closed kitchen door. Taking two steps forward, I fell over the oven door, that had only just then dropped down into the open position in front of me. Holding aloft the chicken with one hand as I fell over, breaking my fall with the other hand on the concrete floor, I felt a sharp pain momentarily within my right shinbone from the edge of the oven door.

After a little cursing and cussing as I lay there in the dark upon the cold concrete floor. I managed to pick myself up, with the well-cooked slippery greasy chicken carcass still held tightly within my other hand above my head. I could feel the juices from the carcass running back down upon my wrist as I held it aloft. Blindly feeling for the oven door with my right hand, I was able to close the door upon standing up. Straining my eyes to become accustomed to the dark, I limped and fumbled my way on past the cooker with an outstretched hand, in the direction of the unseen closed kitchen door. On reaching and feeling for the closed door, I pushed the base of the door open with the toe of my shoe. As the door started slowly to open, and the first crack of light fully appeared around the edges of the door frame, I once again took a huge caveman's bite out of the partly used chicken, and then swallowed the mouth watering tasty bite once again in one gulp. I could taste the tasty juices of the chicken as the overspill ran on down the sides of my mouth. Wiping the grease from my chin with my sleeve arm, I raised my right foot once again to take that single step up into the well-lit kitchen as the door fully opened. Whilst holding the chicken close to my mouth with two hands, I was about to take another huge bite upon entry into the kitchen, just as I noticed that the carcass appeared to have moved. Momentarily, I thought this to be an optical illusion, a trick of the light. On moving the chicken carcass further away from my eyes for a clearer view to what it may have been, I was immediately horrified by what I was now looking at; the chicken had indeed moved, for it was alive with maggots.

Holding the carcass further away from myself with out-stretched arms, I could not see the actual chicken carcass for the squirming mass of maggots. Maggots were dropping everywhere, as I held this living thing further away from my person; they were dropping to the floor in abundance, and trailing back behind myself into the scullery upon the concrete floor. Dropping the moving carcass to the floor with a shudder on immediately becoming violently sick, I could see more of the maggots bouncing from the carcass as it hit the floor about my feet.

My brother, who had caught a glimpse of what was happening, very quickly left the room. No sooner had he disappeared, than the dog reappeared from beneath the kitchen table. The dog, being a faithful old mutt, ran to the moving mass upon the floor just as my old dad entered the kitchen from the adjoining living-room. One look at me being violently sick, and the squirming mess about my feet and my old dad, very quickly disappeared back out of the kitchen to the living-room. The floor about my feet was now in a right mess; the maggots were swimming about the sick as they spread themselves further across the floor like floating rafts in a pond. Looking down upon the mess whilst propping myself up against the kitchen wall with tears streaming down my face, I watched the dog tear into the maggot-infested chicken carcass amid the sick that he himself was now sliding upon. I became very ill and weak at the knees as I again become violently sick. I could see the maggots being thrown back down and out from my own mouth amid the sick, as it fell away from myself and then over the dog that had gotten in the way upon the floor below. Looking back down with wet glistening eyes at the sick covered dog that was now sitting in an upright begging position, I could see the maggot-infested carcass, held tight within his jaws. I then looked to his tail that was wagging at speed. Holding tight to my stomach with both hands, I strained with the violent eruptions that were taking place within the bowels of my stomach with exhausting consequences. On trying not to look at the dog, I could see further maggots dropping on to the floor in abundance from the gaps between the dog's teeth, whilst holding it firmly between its jaws; drooling wet saliva was escalating down from both sides of the dog's sagging soft slobbering mouth mixed with the juices from the greasy chicken carcass. Heaving my heart up at the sight before me, I felt that I had to get away from my present position. In my torment of sickness, I turned to go back into the darkened scullery; on doing so, I once again fell over the oven door that had once again dropped down from its shut position. Whilst sat once again upon the concrete scullery floor, I could see with the help of the light that was emitting itself from the kitchen into the dark scullery, a trail of maggots, that were running from the meat safe to the kitchen door. The dog who had followed me on out and into the scullery, was now sat with the live moving chicken carcass only inches from my face; it was as if he had wanted to share his new-found dinner with me.

With the carcass only inches from my nose, I very quickly picked myself up, and ran to the back door that led on out into the rear garden. On my escape into the garden,

I could see that the moon had only just broken through the dense blackness of the night. The noise that I myself was giving out upon being violently sick, could be heard across the neighbouring gardens. Lights were being switched on within the surrounding houses as the sound from myself being sick echoed about the buildings. Leaning upon an adjoining fence to the rear of the garden, my violent heaving and being sick had started to ease off a little. Feeling a little better, I turned around from the fence to wipe my eyes; on wiping away the sick tears from my eyes, I noticed the dog sitting beside me. Looking at him, I could see that the chicken carcass was still held tight within his jaws with the maggots still dropping to the ground. The sight of the dog had once again started to make me heave; what made matters worse, was the sound of my dear old dad heaving inside the house, as he and my dear old mum started to clean up the mess behind myself; hearing my old dad, and now my dear old mum heaving in the background together, had not helped my present predicament, for I was once again leaning over the fence being sick.

My brother had ventured out into the rear garden to see if he could help me. As I turned momentarily from the fence, I could see that my brother was trying to prize open the dog's jaw with both hands, to get at the infested chicken carcass. Just as my brother had started to push his fingers between the teeth of the tightly shut jaws, the maggots started to drop like rain water once again to the ground. Whilst he was trying to force out the greasy carcass, I looked to the grease, and the saliva that was mixed with the juices from the carcass, as it dripped on down from both sides of the dog's own frothy mouth, and then over the backs of my brother's hands. Upon my brother struggling with the carcass, and with the vice-like grip of the dog, I could see the cocktail of juices upon his hands had now started to run further on down and over his arms. I then looked to the wriggling maggots that were floating about his skin amid the saliva from the dog, as he persisted in recapturing the chicken carcass from the strong jaws of the dog. I immediately turned my head to sick back over a neighbouring garden with an added pain to my stomach. There appeared to be no end to my predicament. Finally, my brother had gotten the chicken carcass away from the dog; on doing so, my brother threw the slimy carcass into the dustbin. Picking up a nearby shovel, my brother set about throwing dirt over all the sick that was spread about the garden. I could still see the cocktail of silvery juices glistening upon the backs of my brother's hands and arms within the bright moonlight, as he went about his business. The dog, who was not amused by the loss of his dinner, had run back into the house with the sulks.

The next day, my dear old dad and mum, had not spoken a word about the incident. I was definitely not a happy person. It took a further three years before I once again tasted a chicken. Upon that brand new day three years later, just as I was about to take a bite from a crispy brown chicken portion, the dog was sat at my feet with wagging tail; he was waiting for me to share the chicken portion with him. However, I did share something with him; the toe of my boot. This was another day and chapter within my life, that I will never forget.

The Kiss in the Dark

In 1964, on 24th May, my wife went into hospital to have our first-born; whilst she was in the hospital, I visited the hospital with my sister. My sister and I returned back late in the evening to my own home, situated in the Outer Circle area of Shirley Warren, Southampton. Upon our return to my home, I could see the two nosy old ladies who lived across the street from myself, peering out from their curtains, from behind their lower front room window. They were both sat in the dark watching our every move as my sister and I approached the front door of my home. It was a very dark evening with little moonlight. The street lighting illuminated the surrounding area outside of my home, and that of the two old ladies across the street, who were peering out of their window, not realising that I could see them. On opening the front door to my home upon our arrival, I said to my sister, 'Don't put the lights on when we enter the house, because the two old ladies who live opposite, are sat in the dark behind their own curtains watching us both.' I then said, 'Just go straight upstairs to the front bedroom.' I further explained to my sister that these nosy old ladies across the road sat within the dark for hours, and they don't miss a thing.

Upon shutting tight the front door, I followed my sister up to the main bedroom that was situated to the front of the house. On entering the main front bedroom, I turned on the light, just as my sister and I walked towards the front bay window. My sister and I could just see both the nosy neighbours looking back up at us, from within their own darkened lower front room window opposite. I then said to my sister, 'Come here, let's give them something to talk about.'

My sister, who was game for a laugh, walked up close to me and placed her arms about my neck in a loving manner; on doing so, she then kissed me about the head. Having my own curtains already drawn wide open, we could see the two old ladies out of the corner of our eyes looking back up at us, as we resumed our position.

My sister did make it look good; she kissed me about the face and head whilst holding me around the neck in full view of the open bedroom window. Upon stretching out an arm as my sister was giving me her loving attention, I switched the bedroom light off. My sister and I could then clearly see the two old ladies below moving closer to the inside of their own window for a better view of what we were doing.

As my sister was kissing me, I stretched out my other arm to slowly draw to a close the curtains. My sister and I then sat in the dark away from the window, for a further half an hour, whilst having a cup of tea and a chat. After we had both drunk our tea, we both decided to go. On leaving the house unseen by means of the back door to the house, my sister and I quietly walked on down the road and out of sight. Ten minutes later, we arrived at my sister's own home that was just around the corner.

The next day I attended the hospital in the afternoon to see my wife and new-born son. Upon my arrival at the hospital, my wife had already been informed about my unfaithfulness, and that I had taken a woman into the main bedroom of her home, where this woman and I had stayed all night. Apparently there had been an anonymous phone call to her from outside the hospital.

My wife still believes today, many years later, that I was

up to no good. I wasn't a happy person. I wonder who could have made that call, that has given me so much grief over the years?

The Plastic Flowers

Many years ago, when I moved house into the area of the Outer Circle, Shirley Warren, Southampton, I once again encountered two nosy old ladies living opposite myself. They were very much like the other two old ladies who had lived opposite my old address in the Sholing area of Southampton. They were both always sat looking out of their window nosing upon all that was going on within the street outside. They too, as the others had done in the past, would take it in turns to comb or brush each other's grey hair, whilst one or the other sat in a chair, looking back out of their window on to the street outside. Having this second set of old ladies living opposite myself, tells me that every street or road across the city must have very similar two old ladies sat within the windows, doing the same old thing. My final conclusion upon this, is that there must be a circle or cult that they all attend at the end of each year, to discuss and to reminisce upon what they have all seen, or done; or further to the point, on just whom they have dobbed into the local council, for these old dears have nothing better to do with their time. In short, they are just nosy old curtain twitchers and busy bodies with diseased minds; it's a wonder that these old dears had any hair left to comb at the end of each year.

Throughout the months, whilst working upon the dust carts in Southampton, I collected all the plastic flowers that I could find from the houses and dustbins upon the daily rounds. These plastic flowers were very new to the media.

There were many people within the public sector who had not seen or heard about the new plastic flowers. In the old days, these plastic flowers were given away singularly to the public upon the purchasing of certain household commodities. Within the first six months of the plastic flowers' appearance, I must have saved fifty or more from the city council dust carts. Upon one dark winter's evening, I pushed the plastic coated wire stems of each separate plastic flower, deep down into the earth all around the garden to the front of my house; after planting all the plastic flowers about the garden, together, they looked very colourful, and made a miserable winter more acceptable to mankind. My front garden, come morning, would definitely look to be the best in the street. I was quite proud of the new look to my front garden.

That same night, snow dropped heavily down upon the gardens and the streets outside. On getting up in the morning, the plastic flowers looked very picturesque, as they stood proudly in an abundance of colours protruding out from the white snow.

Two days later, whilst I was clearing the snow from off my front path, one of the nosy old ladies from the house across the road appeared upon the snow-covered pavement to my home, and asked, 'How is it that your flowers are still in bloom, whilst everyone else's have been and gone?'

Somehow, the two old ladies had missed the replanting of my prized flower arrangements. Upon looking at the nosy old trout standing and looking over my garden fence, I replied, 'I had those flowers especially imported from Russia, they are very tough and sturdy and will only grow in the winter months.'

'That's clever,' she uttered with a voice full of surprise; 'They look very much like the flowers that we grow over here,' she added with a mystified look upon her face. The nosy old lady then walked back across the road to fetch her friend, who was watching from behind the curtains of their own home.

Moments later, both the old ladies had returned to take photographs of my beautiful winter roses, tulips, daffodils and wallflowers etc. They were both full of excitement as they took photograph after photograph of my splendid-looking winter garden.

'Just where did you get them?' asked the friend of the first old lady; 'They are absolutely beautiful,' she added with a wide smile.

I then looked to her and replied, 'A friend brought them back over from Russia; he's in the export and import business.'

Both the nosy old trouts then told me that they both were going to send off to the local nurseries, to see if they too, could import these wonderful looking winter flowers. After the discussion and photographing, the two nosy old ladies walked back across the street to their own home, to resume their position behind the window. I never did know what the outcome of that was. I was a happy person.

The Bottle

Some years ago, I was employed by the Ichen Transport Company as a lorry driver. Their premises at that time were situated within the docklands of the Royal Pier in Southampton. Being a lorry driver for the Ichen Transport Company meant that I was on contract hire to the British American Tobacco Company in Foundry Lane, Southampton; the lorry that I was driving had to be left parked inside the British American Tobacco Company's security compound in Foundry Lane, Millbrook, Southampton for loading. During the day, the lorry was loaded by their own workers with cigarettes and many different types of tobacco, in my absence, for readiness upon that night's night run. In the late evenings, I myself would collect my already loaded vehicle from within their compound, along with the necessary paperwork and destination. On collection of my already loaded lorry, and leaving the security compound, I would be accompanied by two British American Tobacco security men in a white van. The security van spearheaded my valuable cargo all the way to the journey's end.

Upon one winter's evening, there was myself and another driver who was on contract hire from Ichen Transport to the British American Tobacco Company; we both had the same destination run and departure time; the other driver who was on the same night run as I, was my own brother. My brother and I had to drive two separate loaded lorries, fully loaded with the cigarettes and tobacco up to Hurn Airport. From Hurn Airport, a plane would then take on board the cigarettes, and then fly them on to France. The cigarettes normally went by sea, but at that time, the shipping companies had a strike upon their hands. Because of the strike, the delivery of the cigarettes and tobacco to France had to be secretly moved by lorries in the late dark evenings. When driving a load of cigarettes to a given destination, one was not allowed to stop; not even for a cup of tea or a leak.

Driving in convoy upon the main trunk roads in those days at night, was not an easy task; we had to travel in almost total blackness, for the street lighting in those days was almost nil upon the drive to or from the many different towns that we had encountered upon our journey to Hurn Airport. Travelling upon the road, my brother and I had to make full use of our headlights to see our way forward. Driving out of the blackness of the night, one could see each town ahead of ourselves lit up like a Christmas tree. The lights illuminated the black sky with an array of colourful lights, that surrounded the towns like a hazy fog in a delightful way; one would believe that one was about to enter into wonderland with an imaginative multitude of crystal lights, that were sparkling like diamonds high in the big black sky ahead. On driving through each different town upon our journey to Hurn Airport, the trunk roads, would once again become very dark. Not being able to stop upon route, I had drunk a full bottle of lemonade upon my long journey through the night. There were not many motorways in those days; only the trunk roads, that would often taken one on through a network of twisting country-side roads, then back again on to a network of trunk roads.

On our arrival at Hurn Airport, it was very dark. The airport itself was almost in total darkness. There was no moon, just blackness. Following the small white security van, we entered the airport through a gap within a chain link fencing, situated further down a remote part of a country lane. I thought this to be a little strange, entering an airfield through a gap in the fencing in the dead of night. A further thought then entered into my head the moment we followed the white security van on through the gap in the fencing; why not the main gate? Perhaps there was a picket at the main entrance; who knows? All my brother and I could do was to follow the leader for fear of getting lost in the blackness of the night. I had to follow the security van's rear lights, with my brother in turn following mine in almost pitch darkness. There was no sign of runway lights, or any other lights as we moved blindly onwards. We were now driving upon what appeared to be open fields; we could now only see a carpet of grass looming back up at us to the front of our bright headlights as we all travelled in single file in the blackness of the night. It seemed more like a mystery tour of the unseen airport, then that of a normal delivery job. If it were not for the rear lights on the security van that we were following, my brother and I would have lost our directions to the off-loading zone.

As we followed each other's tail lights, an airport police van materialised from nowhere. They stopped the white security van to the front of us; we were all told to switch off the headlights and to drive on sidelights only; we were then told to continue following each other's tail lights. The white security van was now in close pursuit behind the airport police with my brother and I following close behind. On following each other's tail lights, I could just see through the blackness upon the ground to the front of myself, that we were now travelling upon what I presumed to be a tarmac runway. Finally, upon reaching the off-loading point, which was to the centre of nowhere, my lorry was off-loaded under the cover of darkness on to a plane. The lighting around the airport for loading the plane was very poor indeed. The plane was but a ghostly shadow upon the ground amid a wide black area of the airfield.

There were no buildings of any kind in view, just an emptiness that was filled with blackness. If it were not for following the airport police and the white security van to the off-loading point, my brother and I would not have found the plane; or even have known that we were situated somewhere upon an airfield.

The airport police reminded us at all times that this was a contract of strict secrecy; had the striking seamen known of this transporting of tobacco by plane, all hell would have broken loose. I felt as if I were a part of an unofficial smuggling ring, it was all very hush-hush. We were like gangsters working throughout the night under the cover of darkness.

The night was very still, and very quiet. The crewmen who were unloading and reloading went about their jobs in almost total silence. Had this have been the making of a film, the location, and the blanket of darkness, and the ghostly fogged light that surrounded the silver plane, would have been the ideal setting.

It was now about two o'clock in the morning, and my brother and I were getting very tired whilst waiting around for the airport crewmen to off-load the valuable consignment on to the plane. Finally, after the plane was fully loaded, the plane took off for France. As the plane slowly took off, we all stood in the dark upon the runway watching the plane's night lights slowly disappearing into the black sky. The plane's carrying capacity had only allowed for one consignment load at a time; we all had to wait until morning for the plane's return before my brother's lorry could be unloaded.

After the plane had disappeared out of sight, my brother and I decided to move my empty lorry away from the unloading zone, whilst my brother's lorry was being guarded by the two security men until the plane's return. My brother and I entered the cab of my lorry. After starting the engine, and against the regulations of the airport, I switched on my headlights to full beam, and then drove the empty lorry away from the unloading area, into an unknown direction to look for accommodation. As we drove at five miles per hour through the blackness of the night, I looked to my brother who was sat somewhere within the passenger seat next to myself; it was so dark, I could not even see his face. We both decided that we had to leave the airfield somehow; but how? We hadn't a clue to where the hole in the fencing that we both had previously entered through was situated. As we drove further along in the pitch blackness of the night, we got ourselves completely lost and out of touch with all humanity; we could see no signs that might direct us away from or off the airfield, and into the direction of a nearby town. As we drove a little further, I was confident that we were now out of the airport and somewhere upon an open road, even though there were no other vehicle lights to be seen. We both looked for the illumination of town lights in the black sky but to no avail.

Deciding not to go any further, just in case we could not find our way back to the off-loading zone, we stopped the lorry to assess our present predicament; we decided there and then, that we were going to have a sleep. There was no moon, nothing for the pair of us to see exactly where we where parked. After switching off the engine and then the lights, we both listened to the quiet of the night in total blackness. Moments later, we both left the cab to climb up upon the rear of the lorry. On doing so, we both crawled under the sheeting that hung down from the wood-panelled bulk head, that was situated behind the cab like half a tent. In the stillness of the night, we could only hear each other's voices, or feel an accidental touch upon each other's hand as we both fumbled our way around in the pitch dark. It had now gotten very cold and windy as we both went under the lorry's sheet for a sleep. Under the sheeting, my brother and I snuggled down for the remainder of the night.

Two minutes after getting ourselves settled under the sheeting for a long overdue sleep, I was re-awakened by the sound of voices. On giving my brother a shake, I whispered, 'There's someone outside.'

Just as I had spoken, someone on the outside was trying to knock upon the sheeting as if it were a front door. The night outside was as dark as it was inside. On hearing the voices, and someone trying to knock on the front door, my brother and I simultaneously poked out our heads from under the sheet and said together, 'Who's there?'

From out of the blackness a torch brightly shone into both our eyes. 'You under there?' came a voice from behind the torch.

My brother and I could then see the silhouettes of what appeared to be three male persons moving about at the entrance to our make-shift tent. 'What's going on?' asked my brother.

'Do you know exactly where you have parked?' shouted one of the men.

It was only then that my brother and I recognised the three persons as airport police.

I replied, protecting my eyes from the light of the torch, 'No!'

'Get the fuck out of here now!' boomed another voice.

'You're parked in the middle of an airfield!' shouted another.

'If we had not seen your headlights being switched off, we wouldn't have known that you were here, *now get the fuck out!*' remarked another.

My brother and I fell from the rear of the lorry to the ground in our haste with a thud. Upon jumping to our feet, we both searched blindly for the outside cab door handles.

On finding the door handles with the help of an unintentional waver of light that flashed from one of the policemen's torches, we both opened the doors to the cab; after climbing up into the cab, we were soon on the move.

'Follow me!' shouted one of the airport policemen as he switched on his flashing police lights upon his vehicle. My brother and I followed the flashing blue lights behind the police van for ten minutes until we came to the wide gap in the chain link fencing. The gap in the fencing took us back on to a very dimly lit country lane whence we had first entered. Stopping upon the country lane, one of the airport policeman said, 'Look! We know who you are, and what you're up here for, just follow this lane and you will come to a town. You will find an overnight station there if you need a room.'

After listening to the airport policeman who had given us both a gentle smack upon the wrist for parking without lights on a runway, we drove off down the country lane. On driving around a bend that had towering trees to both sides of the road, my brother and I could see the lights from the town ahead of ourselves. It did not take us too long to find a rented room. The night was now very short.

In the morning, we were both still very tired after having only four hours' sleep. On our return to the airport, we found that my brother's lorry was now empty and waiting for him. Climbing up into the cab, my brother started up the engine. We both left the airport in the direction of home. Upon our long journey back to base I followed my brother all the way, as I was not too familiar with the return route. On driving through one of the unfamiliar towns, I found myself in need of a piss; I tried desperately to get my brother's attention as he drove his lorry ahead of me, to no avail. Not being able to stop for fear of losing my brother *en route*, I found myself holding very tightly to the steering wheel, with the pain of my bladder at bursting point.

Looking down upon the seat next to myself, in what was now daylight I could see the discarded empty lemonade bottle that I had thrown upon the seat upon my journey up to the airport; picking the empty lemonade bottle up, I then decided to piss in the bottle whilst driving along the main road. Whilst still driving along the busy main road behind my brother's lorry, I took out my baby-making machine with one hand whilst holding the steering wheel with the other. Having the bottle jammed tightly between my knees, I started to piss into the narrow neck of the lemonade bottle with great difficulty. The head of my love tool was much bigger then the neck of the bottle.

Having one eye upon my brother's lorry to the front of myself for fear of losing sight of him, and trying to piss into the narrow bottle neck whilst on the move, was not an easy task. I managed to do a little at a time as I ran with the traffic. As I did so, the piss cascaded down the outside of the bottle and back over my hand. Stopping at a red traffic light with my brother now ahead of myself and out of sight, I continued to finish off what I was trying to do; holding tight the bottle between my wet knees in my now stable position, I re-guided my baby-making machine back into the bottle with my left hand, whilst holding the narrow neck of the bottle with my right hand. I then continued to fill the bottle to the very top. Having the cab of my lorry rather high up from the road when I stopped at the traffic lights made it almost impossible for any other person upon the outside to see what I was doing. Filling the bottle to the very top, I found that the one bottle was not really going to be enough; I was still bursting at the seams. The right hand that was holding the narrow neck of the bottle between my knees had gotten rather wet with the overspill. The bottle itself was now very slippery to hold. Whilst still waiting at a red traffic light, I was just about to place the top back on the bottle when the lights turned green. Suddenly, with the hand brake firmly pulled up into the holding position, the empty lorry had jolted approximately one foot forward with a thud and a hefty jerk. Upon the lorry jolting forwards, the bottle slipped out of my hand and momentarily spilt its full contents all over my trousers, down my legs, over my shoes, and then down upon the floor of the cab about my feet. I momentarily looked at the mess below myself in bewilderment and then at the discarded used match sticks that were floating about my feet like logs in a pond. I was not a happy person.

I then realised that some person had crashed into the rear of my lorry, just as the lights had turned green. After redressing myself, I jumped out and down from my cab to the road surface; as I walked towards the rear of the lorry, my saturated socks within my shoes started to give out a slopping sound. People within stationary cars and upon the sidewalk could see that I was awash with water to my lower half, and that I was leaving very wet footprints behind myself on walking to the rear of the lorry. On reaching the rear of the lorry, the traffic lights had once again turned back to red whilst I was investigating the cause of the lorry jolting forward in such an unexpected manner. On my approach, I could see a man sat within a car behind the steering wheel; looking at him, I could see that he was laughing and pointing to the rear end of my lorry. Upon reaching the rear end of my lorry, I looked to see what he was laughing and pointing to. I then looked under the rear end of my lorry as there was nothing to see. I was then amazed to see a small German Messerschmitt bubble car jammed under the rear chassis of the lorry; the driver was an old man wearing a trilby hat; he was sitting in an upright position looking out of his unbroken front windscreen to the rear axle upon my lorry. The bed of my lorry had an approximate three foot overhang, before one could see the rear of his car tucked right in under the rear chassis.

I then shouted to him, 'What on earth are you doing under there?'

The old man, without looking left or right of himself, put his car into reverse, then very slowly reversed the car back out from under the rear of my lorry. Having gotten himself out from under, the old man quietly continued to sit within his car in a motionless upright position, with his eyes still looking out of the front windscreen in the direction of my rear axle. I then looked at the slightly flattened roof just as all the other drivers in the queue started to roar with laughter. I stood there looking at this old man for a moment, then watched him slowly sink his head and neck back down into his own shoulders with embarrassment.

Leaving him to his embarrassment, I walked back to the cab of my lorry with wet feet still slopping within my shoes. Climbing back aboard, I set myself in readiness for take off. The traffic lights had now changed to green for the umpteenth time, so I proceeded to drive off in a rather wet but composed manner. As I again travelled with the flow of the traffic, I once again took out my baby-making machine to finish off what I had started; but this time, I did not use the bottle, I just let the piss run on down to join the rest of the puddle at my feet. Further down the road, I found my brother waiting at the kerbside; he was stood upon the kerbside asking where I had been. I explained to him what had happened. My brother roared with laughter as he climbed back into his own cab. We both then continued back to base.

The Bus Ride

At the age of twenty-six, I had the worst bus ride that any one person could ever have encountered; it was a bus ride that was full of embarrassment. Upon one very hot sunny day in the month of August, I boarded the number five bus that was on route to the Southampton city centre from Sholing. This number five double-decker bus was in those days the longest bus ride on the route. I sat on the upper deck upon the left-hand side, four seats back from the front window. As it travelled the route, the bus stopped at every bus-stop upon that journey into town. Every time the bus stopped to drop off passengers, I could see clearly from the upper window long queues waiting to board as others got off. The bus itself was packed tight with commuters; finding a place upon the bus was not an easy task. The bus was very soon over-crowded with all seats taken; it was now standing room only. This bus left queues of disgruntled and dissatisfied commuters at every bus-stop; standing room only, by law, allowed only a specified amount of commuters to stand within the aisles. On that day of my journey to town, the driver must have been oblivious to the law; the commuters were not only standing like squashed sardines along the lower deck, holding tight to the leather straps that were situated upon rails above their heads, they also overspilled one behind the other, standing all the way up the stairs. Upon the upper deck, the situation was very much the same as the deck below; the commuters had overspilled the top stairs and the upper aisles like squashed sardines, they also held tight to the straps provided upon the upper railings along both sides of the aisle; the only empty seat upon the top deck was next to myself. I was completely mystified as to why the seat next to myself was not taken by another commuter.

From time to time I looked up at the nearest faces that were looking back down at myself, as they held tight to the straps above their heads. Upon their faces were fixed, unmoving, serious, glaring eyes staring right back at myself. Looking away from the staring eyes, I continued to peer out of the window at the passing houses below as we slowly journeyed onwards.

The day was very hot; it was so hot that parts of the vinyl seating were too hot to touch by hand; the sun's magnification through the windows was immense. Once again, I slowly turned my head to look up at the nearest commuter still standing by the empty seat beside myself; as I glanced up, I could see that a male commuter was still looking back down upon myself, with a look that could kill; I then looked to the others who were standing quite close to him; they too were looking down upon me with the same fixed unmoving look, with glaring penetrating eyes. Somewhat bewildered, I looked at my reflection in the window. Whilst looking at my reflection, I searched my own image to see if there was anything about my person that may have offended them; I could see nothing wrong. I just could not understand why the seat next to myself was not being occupied. Looking down at the empty seat beside myself, I searched with my eyes to see if there was some-thing spilt upon the seat; having done that, I then brushed my hand across the hot vinyl seating; again, I could find nothing there. Looking waist-high between the commuters who were standing within the aisle near to the empty seat beside myself, I could see between their bodies and limbs two old ladies, who were peering back at me from the opposite seat; I then looked back up at the commuters who were still standing beside the empty seat, I could see no change in their expressions as they all continued to stare back down at myself. On glancing once again back out of the window, I could feel their eyes on my person; there was hardly a sound to be heard, even though the bus was completely packed; it was as if every person on board knew something that I didn't. Looking at all the people upon the bus was like looking at a video with the sound turned off; the silence that had clouded the upper deck was unbelievable.

The bus once again came to a stop; two of the commuters who were standing alongside the empty seat next to myself, had reached their destination; they slowly moved along the queue within the aisle behind each other, and then on down the stairs to get off the bus. After the two commuters had gotten off the bus with a few others, I looked up from the window to see if the next in line were looking back down at myself; they were. As the bus pulled away from its stop, I could see, upon looking up, an old lady who was holding tight to the overhead leather hand strap beside the empty seat; held under her other arm was an almost full shopping bag; in her hand, upon the same arm, was another full shopping bag; I could see that she was struggling to hold her standing position, and that she had no intention of sitting down beside myself within the empty seat. Looking at her, I could see that she too was now giving me an unusual look of contempt with glaring eyes, just as the other commuters had done before her. I then looked down with guilt at the seat for some unforeseen reason. Again, on seeing nothing wrong with the seat, I looked back up to where the two old ladies were still peering over at me from in between the limbs of the standing commuters; they were both sat staring at myself, with a fixed glare, and faces like prunes. Both the old ladies then started to whisper to each other. Upon whispering to each other they both looked back at myself, with an obvious objection to my presence; I then looked back to the window at my own reflection; I still could not understand why no other person would take the seat. The bus stopped again, more people had gotten off, fewer boarded. Once again, the bus continued onwards. For some unknown reason, the journey to town seemed to take for ever.

The commuters had now started to thin out upon each bus-stop that followed. The aisle within the upper deck was now clear of standing commuters. Mystified as to what had been happening, I looked to the right of myself in the direction of the aisle beside the empty seat, I could clearly see the two old ladies opposite, who were still looking straight at me with contempt.

As I neared my destination, I noticed most of the seats were now empty. My long journey upon that bus was now almost at an end; I had only one more stop to go. Looking out of the window, I could see that my stop was not too far away. Placing each of my hands separately upon the hot red vinyl seating either side of my hips, I positioned myself in readiness to push myself up out of the seat; whilst I paused in my present position to await the slowing down of the bus, the two old ladies opposite were trying to stand up with great difficulty to meet their destination; they were both struggling very hard to get out from their seating, but their own oversized body weight, their shopping bags, and their heavy oversized overcoats despite the heat of the day, slowed them both down.

When the two old ladies had finally got themselves out of their seat, they both stood within the aisle with their bags in hand looking back down at myself with the same old look of disapproval. As the bus slowed down a little more, both the old ladies moved on down the aisle towards the stairs. I too started to get up and out of my seat for the very same stop. Pushing upon my hands to help myself up out of the seat, I looked down to the red vinyl seating that was showing between my parted knees; I then felt rather embarrassed and shocked by what my own eyes had just fallen upon. I had found the answer as to why no other person wanted to sit in the seat next to me. With disbelief, I could see laid there upon the seat, as if fast asleep, my baby-making machine! I could have died there and then. I had no underpants on, and there was a hole in my jeans that allowed my love tool to sunbathe itself upon the warm red vinyl seating. Very quickly upon standing up, I pushed my baby-making machine back on through the hole in my jeans whence it came. After I had redressed my person, I walked down the aisle towards the stairs.

On descending to the bottom of the stairs behind the two old ladies, the bus had only just come to a full stop. Standing behind the two old ladies as they waited for the exit doors to open, I looked to the driver, who in turn gave to me a peculiar look. Upon the doors opening, other commuters and the two old ladies had gotten off the bus, followed closely by myself. As the bus pulled away, the bus driver gave to me another peculiar look, then a smile. I felt terrible, obviously a complaint had been made to the driver, worse still not one person, had given to me some sort of nudge, just to let me know of my unforeseen embarrassing situation.

This extraordinary unexpected embarrassment had made me feel rather uncomfortable. As I walked along the pavement towards the town centre, I felt as if every person who passed me by knew about my love tool being fast asleep upon the seat of that number five bus. I was not a happy person. As I walked further away from the bus-stop, I could see the two old ladies both still looking back at myself, as they walked across the city park. I could also see that they were both still obviously talking about my predicament aboard the number five bus. Ever since that unforgettable and embarrassing day I have worn under-pants.

The Fight

When I was twenty-four years of age, I was walking on my own on the pavement down a road called Pound Tree Road, into the direction of St Mary's Street, near to the Kingsland Square market place in Southampton. I had just left the town centre after an evening out, and was on my way back home. The route that I was to take home led me into a situation that I was not prepared for. It was about ten o'clock in the evening, upon a very dark winter's night, when an unexpected occurrence placed yet another chapter of a strange but true adventure into my charmed life.

I was at the time walking along Pear Tree Road towards the T-road of St Mary's Street, with the Kingsland Square market place to the right of myself. I could see a large crowd of people approximately fifty yards ahead of myself surrounded by light from a street lamp. I could also see that they were gathering and standing upon the pavement, on the other side of the crossroad, outside a pub. Some of the crowd were standing in the gutter, with a few more in the middle of the road. They were all illuminated against the blackness of the night by the street lighting and the lights from a nearby public house. It was obvious to me, even from fifty yards, that they had all just momentarily stepped out from the public house. They were all standing in St Mary's Street, looking back up the road into the direction of the Six Dials. There was a deathly silence on my final approach. They were but a shadow of a crowd looking into the darker part of the road ahead of themselves. This was in the very same direction of my left turn out of Pear Tree Road, towards the Six Dials and my route home.

Seeing this shadowy crowd ahead of myself whilst walking towards them upon the pavement in Pear Tree Road, I widened my steps to see exactly what they were all looking at around the corner, this being my next left turning. Coming now out of Pear Tree Road upon my left turn into St Mary's Street in the direction that the crowd was still looking, I could see a shadowy figure chasing another upon the pavement. As my eyes adjusted to the very dim lighting in St Mary's Street upon my left turn, I could see that it was a man giving chase to a woman into an entrance of a closed shop doorway. Within the shop doorway, the man was giving the woman a terrible beating upon the floor; she then managed to get up, then run to the next shop screaming, just as the man again chased her into that same shop doorway. Her screams upon being beaten echoed throughout the still air of the night. The woman then got up from off the floor and ran to the next shop doorway screaming, with her attacker in close pursuit. They were running from shop to shop towards the Six Dials away from myself and the onlooking crowd. Turning to look behind myself at the shadowy onlookers, I was appalled to see so many doing nothing about it. To me, they had no sense of chivalry. They seemed to be happy to watch a woman in distress; a woman who was being beaten to within an inch of her life. I considered the onlookers to be cowards. I then turned my head back in the direction that I was walking, only to see the two shadowy figures still running in and out of the many different shop doorways ahead of myself, with her screaming at the top of her voice, as she tried desperately to elude her pursuer. Upon the woman being caught by her pursuer, I could see this man beating her about the head and body as she lay upon the ground outside yet another shop doorway; she was covered in blood. Somehow, the woman had managed to stand upon her own two feet, and then in desperation, run into the next shop doorway to escape the fury that he was raining upon her with blows from his huge fist. The man repeated his every move within each shop doorway that the woman entered into for her own salvation. I had now seen enough, I could not understand whence this woman was obtaining her strength. He was like a man possessed! The woman was now giving out an ear-piercing, deathly, frightening scream, as he continuously beat her about the body. Her screams were bouncing back off the walls of the surrounding buildings upon both sides of the road, as it echoed throughout the dark still night. Now moving quickly forward to give assistance, I confronted the man just as he was beating her once again upon the floor of a shop doorway. I shouted to the man to leave her alone. The woman was screaming hysterically, her person was badly bruised and bleeding profusely. The man, who was bending over her and raining blows about her head with his huge fist, very quickly upon my confrontation, stood up straight; he then turned from the woman laid upon the ground to face me.

Bravely, I stood my ground and said to him, 'Leave her alone or you will get the same.'

The man, who was slightly smaller than me, but built like a tank, momentarily stood looking straight at me, holding one hand in his inside coat pocket. I did not know out of the two of us, who was the more surprised upon my confrontation at the scene of his brutal attack. I could not believe what was to follow; the man pulled his hand back out from his inside coat pocket, and then started to wave an object close to my face. It was an object that I had only seen in a comic. What he held within his hand, I thought to have been a myth. But there it was, as large as life. What I was looking at, was a small, sand-filled, leather cosh with patterned criss-crosses adorning both sides. It was something out of a gangster film. The man was waving this thing right in front of my eyes as he said, 'If you come near me, I will hit you with this!'

I looked at him, with a full awareness of the situation and replied, 'Put it away! Or I'll shove it up your arse.'

The man again just stood there for a moment looking at me. He then pushed the cosh back into his inside coat pocket upon turning away from me; I then watched in amazement as he ran across the road to a street called Jail Street.

I looked to the woman upon the floor to give her a helping hand; but then, another unbelievable surprise was to follow; the woman suddenly jumped up from the ground, then ran screaming at the top of her voice down Jail Street in pursuit of her attacker. As she chased her violent attacker on down Jail Street, she screamed, 'Jack! Jack! Come back, Jack!'

Once again, I just stood there in sheer amazement and disbelief at what was now happening. As I stood there with an open mouth, I watched them both disappearing into the darkness of the night down Jail Street, with her still in close pursuit shouting, 'Jack! Jack! Come back!'

I then looked back down the street to where the onlookers were standing; they were nowhere to be seen. The street was now totally empty, there was not another soul to be seen. All that was left was the strange sudden quietness of the night, and the empty dimly-lit streets; with myself, who was now standing like a prat upon the pavement outside a shop doorway. I wasn't a happy person. After standing there for a few moments to gather my senses, I started to walk towards the Six Dials, in the direction of home. After that unexplained situation, I swore to myself, never again.

The Picture House

Between the ages of ten and fourteen, all my old school chums who lived in the same street as myself, used to come around to my house for my cousin and I, every Friday and Saturday evening. The reason why all my chums within the street called at my home upon those two all-important evenings was because it was well known to all our friends that I had it down to a fine art, to be able to open the exit doors of a cinema with a rounded piece of wire.

Upon one Friday evening, seven of my chums and I decided that we were all going to the cinema. The cinema that we all decided upon was the old Plaza in the Northam Road area of Southampton. Today, the old Plaza is now a television company called the Meridian; before that, it was called the Southern Television Centre.

Sneaking into the back door of the Plaza Cinema was the in thing in those days; money was in short supply. The Plaza Cinema had two toilets upon the ground floor; one for the women, and one for the men. Both toilets also had an emergency exit that led back out on to the road. The ladies' toilet, was situated to the left of the big screen, and the men's, to the right of the big screen. These emergency exits were the magic doors into the cinema.

Upon one dark winter's evening, all my friends and I had agreed to meet each other on the road, just outside one of the cinema's exit doors; the exit door that we had chosen to enter into the cinema by led into the ladies' toilets. The ladies' toilets was the easier exit door to open between the two from the outside. Both the exit doors had two single doors that buffed together when shut; the doors had a push-down hand rail upon the inside in order for the doors to open. To open the exit door from the outside, I had to push the rounded piece of wire on through the centre joining crack, where the two doors met when closed; the wire, coming on through from the outside, would then catch upon the inner push-down bar on the inside; on pulling the wire down, the exit door would then open. After successfully opening the exit door from the outside, we all very quietly crept in through the now open door to the inside. Upon closing the doors behind us, we would then be standing in a small hallway; to the left of ourselves was the inner door to the ladies' toilet; to the right was a set of swing doors leading into the cinema. On the other side of those swing doors were two very heavy thick black curtains, which kept the light from going into the cinema from the ladies' toilets. One by one, we all crept on in through the swing doors to hide behind the big black heavy curtains; at a given point in time, when the film upon the big screen had darkened down, two, or three of my chums would then creep out from behind the curtain in a crouched position, in order to get to the nearest empty seats available. Others would crawl upon their hands and knees across the aisles whilst the lights were down low, so's not to be seen by a ticket holder, who might report seeing them coming out of the ladies' toilet.

Upon one winter's night, whilst all my chums had found themselves each a vacant seats within the dark cinema, I thought that my cousin and I were the only ones left in hiding behind the big black curtain. But I was wrong. Whilst waiting for my own chance to make that final dash from behind the big curtain into an empty seat, I felt what I then believed to have been my cousin's arm touching my own beside myself. I then had the strangest feeling that something was not right. When the lights had brightened a little upon the big screen, I pushed the curtain outwards and away from myself to allow a morsel of light to flicker back in upon the person who was standing next to me. Upon doing so, I caught a glimpse of light reflecting back from the peak of a cap. On pushing the big black heavy curtain further out from the two of us, to allow more light in, I had one of the biggest shocks of my life; it was the doorman! The doorman was a very short person, and was well known to all us lads for his running speed. In height, he was approximately four foot nine, and was not a person to mess with. He looked very much like Quasimodo, the hunchback of Notre Dame; he had a very large hump upon his back; he even ran like Quasimodo. Upon seeing the doorman's smiling face looking back up at me from under the shiny peak of his cap, I very quickly vacated my present position; I ran like a bat out of hell from behind the big black curtain, into the semi-darkened picture house. The doorman was right behind me. He was also an expert with the throwing of his large rubber torch; I have never known him to miss a target once he had a person within his sights; his aim was always straight and true.

As I ran to escape the wrath of his flying torch, I shouted out loud within the darkened cinema that was packed tight with people, 'Run lads! It's Quasimodo!'

Just as I shouted from out of the dark amid the flickering film, his big rubber torch hit the back of my head with a thud. The well aimed flying torch sent me tumbling to the floor; I had an almost immediate lump appear to the back of my head, equal in size to an egg. I was not a happy person. Before the doorman could finish me off, I was able to roll over then spring back up upon my own two feet within moments of his lethal weapon striking the rear of my head; I then dashed to the other side of the semi-darkened picture house towards the men's toilet, this being another exit out on to the road. After I shouted, 'Run lads!' all my old chums were running blindly in all directions. Because it was so dark, several of my old chums had run into each other in their haste to escape the flying torch. On reaching the other side of the cinema, I could see the silhouettes of all my chums trying to make their escapes towards the same exit amongst the crowded ticket-paying customers. There were so many of us running around in the dark to escape the fury of Quasimodo, we could not help but to stumble over each other, time after time. Some of the lads whom I bumped into within the dark, I had never seen before. We were all running around the semi-dark cinema like headless chickens. Ticket-paying customers were in an uproar as we had fallen over a few of them time after time during our escape. Making good my own escape to the outside, I turned to look behind myself; I could not believe who had followed me out through the exit door of the gents' toilet. Looking back behind myself, I was shocked to see approximately twenty other lads, unconnected to any of my own friends, pouring out of the exit door. I then stood in further amazement and disbelief, as I then watched all my friends running out of the gents' toilet behind the unknown lads like bats out of hell. Upon watching my friends running for their lives out of the exit door, I could see Quasimodo the doorman, who was almost upon the heels of the last one out. I then fell about laughing, as I thought about the seven of us sneaking in, and now twenty-eight being chased out; it was hilarious. It was like watching a *Carry-On* film. We might not have been able to see the film that night, but we sure did have a good laugh over it.

The night that we were all chased out from the cinema did not deter us from trying again; there were many other nights to follow after that hilarious night; there were also nights when we had all sat snugly within the seats watching a film. Those nights must have been Quasimodo's nights off.

The Embarrassment

Part One

Many years ago, I was employed as a lorry driver by the Pollocks and Browns scrap-yard. Pollocks and Browns's scrap-yard was situated in Princes Street, Northam, Southampton. Upon one hot summer's day, I was standing upon a pile of scrap iron, that was situated upon the rear of my lorry awaiting its off-loading; whilst I stood waiting upon the pile of scrap iron for the very large crane to swing its jib over and above my head for the load's removal, I was trying to bend over by hand, a length of bed iron that was protruding skywards upon the very top of the load. The length of bed iron was attached to one corner of an eight by four sheet of flat tin; whilst I was standing upon this sheet of flat tin, I started to push and pull upon the protruding skyward length of bed iron with both hands, in order to snap it off. As I did so, the sheet of flat tin underfoot started to slide upon the scrap iron that was situated beneath it. On noticing that I was also now sliding along with it, I held on tightly to the protruding length of bed iron even tighter with both hands for fear of falling off; the sheet of tin, with myself still on board, started to move more rapidly over the surface scrap iron towards the driving side of the lorry's side gate as opposed to that of the rear tail gate; it was like being upon a sledge with no brakes. There was no stopping this unexpected journey, and there was nothing that I could do about it. As I momentarily neared the side edge of the lorry upon the scrap iron, I lost my grip upon the length of bed iron; the sheet of tin beneath my feet suddenly disappeared. The sheet of flat tin continued to sail onwards and away from the top of the lorry without me; I descended towards the side gate of the lorry in fear of my life; the lorry's side gate had gone immediately between my legs; I was now momentarily balancing upon the edge of the side gate with one leg on the inside bed of the lorry between the scrap iron, whilst the other leg was hanging down upon the outside; the pain between my groin was immense. I was not a happy person. After landing momentarily upon the side gate, I then continued my fall to the ground. Standing nearby and watching was my future father-in-law. My future father-in-law was also the yard foreman and the first-aid man. On my picking myself up, he asked, 'Are you all right?'

Holding my crutch with both hands, I replied with a squeaky voice, 'Yes! I will be all right in just a minute or so.'

The pain in my groin started to ease off after approximately twenty minutes. Whilst other workers in the yard started to off-load the lorry, I left the scene of my accident to enter into the nearby toilets; I set about having a jimmy widdle; as I was having this jimmy widdle, I had felt something pop inside my baby-making machine as I held it within my hand. Looking down at my bruised love-making tool, I had a bit of a shock; it was not only urine that I was letting go, there was also a stream of blood cascading out amid the urine; it was very frightening.

Very quickly, I picked up from off the floor a dirty cleaning rag, in order to try and stem the flow of blood; wrapping the dirty cleaning rag over the end of my manhood somehow managed to stop the flow totally. Tidying myself up, I walked out of the toilets with great concern at what had just happened. Outside the toilets, I once again encountered my future father-in-law; I told him what had just happened within the toilets; my future father-in-law asked, 'Can I have a look?'

Being my future father-in-law, and I not wanting him to see what his daughter was already getting, I replied, 'No!'

My future father-in-law then as a first-aid man, advised me to attend the hospital. Two hours later, this being whilst on overtime at eight in the evening, I decided that he was right, even though the pain in my groin was almost gone, and there was no sign of any further bleeding.

On reaching the old South Hant's hospital in South-ampton, I entered the building by a side door to the Casualty Department; I had to walk down a very long and narrow corridor; half-way down this corridor, I found the reception counter upon my right. There was no other person to be seen within the corridor other than an old lady on the other side of the counter.

'Can I help you?' said a voice, as I looked up and down the empty corridor.

Turning my head to face the owner of the voice, I re-plied nervously, 'Yes! I have hurt myself down below.'

The old lady receptionist, then asked me in detail, how did the injury occur? What type of injury was it etc. After taking down all the required information, the receptionist leaned over the counter, then pointed with a pencil into the direction that she had wanted me to go; she then said, 'Go to the end of this corridor, through the double doors, then you will see a big waiting-room; wait there, and someone will come to see you.'

Leaving the counter, I walked on down the corridor until I reached a set of swing doors; pushing open the swing doors, I entered a very big waiting-room; looking around the waiting-room, I saw rows and rows of empty seats. There was not a soul to be seen; the silence was deafening.

Helping myself to a seat, I sat down to read a magazine; after ten minutes of waiting, in came this young woman wearing a white coat. 'Mr Johnson?' she asked, whilst holding a folder under her left arm.

'Yes!' I replied upon standing up.

'Will you please follow me,' she asked, as she simultaneously turned to enter a small room beside the swing doors.

On entering into the very small room behind her, the lady in the white coat said, 'Will you please take off all your clothes, and then jump up on to the bed please!'

Feeling rather embarrassed by where my injury was positioned, I asked, 'Where's the doctor?'

'Don't worry about the doctor! Just get your clothes off, and jump up on to the bed,' she replied with a very soft voice and a smile.

I then stood looking at her for a moment before asking, 'Do you want me to take off my socks?'

'Yes! And your socks,' she answered upon leaving the room with yet another smile.

I did not like having a woman attending to my injury, especially having an injury in such a sensitive area upon my person; but I had no choice but to follow orders. Almost immediately after she left the room, I took off all of my clothes before jumping up on to the bed with a rubber sheet across my lap. I could see no point in taking off my socks.

After sitting upon the bed and waiting for five minutes or so, the young woman reappeared. 'Where's the doctor?' I asked again.

'I am the doctor!' she replied, placing the folder on the table. 'Take your socks off! Then lie back further on the bed,' she snapped.

After taking off my socks, I lay back upon the bed.

'Put your legs up! And then look towards the wall,' she ordered as she neared my bruised baby-making machine.

After inspecting my injury, the lady doctor turned to face me whilst my baby-making machine lay upon the inner part of my leg as if it had died.

'I'm afraid you will have to come into hospital for a short while,' she remarked, as she picked up the file to write down a few notes.

'Why?' I asked with puzzlement.

The doctor then turned to look at me once again as she then explained, 'Between your penis and your rectum there is a very fine vein; it looks all right now, but you will have to stay in overnight for observation. We have to make sure that you have not pierced the vein; if you have, this would mean an operation, I'm afraid,' she added, with concern.

'Okay!' I replied uneasily.

I was in that hospital for three days and two nights; I had to drink loads of water to make sure that the vein was not blocked or pierced. I was, however, at the end of those three days, in the clear.

This is not the end of the story. Up till now, the story that you have just read is nothing on its own. All most pointless, one might say; but if you read on, you will find that the story you have just read connects with the next short story following, thus making both stories into one; it's almost like two different ends of a conversation joined together to make one story, but believe me, these two different stories do truly connect to make one true story. Bearing in mind the first story together with this second short story will make interesting reading. You will find that both stories marry in truth, as you near the end of part two.

The Embarrassment
Part Two

A few months later, I was playing football with some of the lads; but unfortunately, the ball went over a fence; on jumping over the fence to retrieve the ball, I caught my trousers by the flies upon a nail situated on the other side of the fence. The nail held me in a stationary fixed position, upside down upon the fence; I was well and truly stuck. This nail ripped through my trousers, thus injuring once again my manhood. It was just after seven in the evening when my unfortunate accident occurred and it was getting rather dark. I asked the other lads to help me down from off the fence; after being helped off the nail by my good chums, I appeared to be all right after a few moments of pain. We then decided, as it was now getting dark, we would now pack in playing football and walk back down the road to the Angus café for refreshments. The Angus café was a local café in Shirley Road, Southampton. Whilst we were all sat down in this café having a cup of tea, I said to my brother, who was talking to one of the lads, that I was going down the road to the public toilets, as there were no toilets for public use within the café. Upon leaving the café, it did not take me too long to enter the public toilets that was situated down the road. In the toilets, I started to have a jimmy widdle; on looking down at my manhood, I could see blood upon my hand; I was now very concerned by what I might have done to myself. Upon further inspection of my love tool, I could see that I had split the join around the base of the helmet to the adjoining foreskin, I immediately placed a piece of clean toilet paper between the helmet and the foreskin to stop the bleeding. After tidying myself up, I left the toilets to go back to the café. On entering back into the café, I told my brother what I discovered within the toilets. My brother then pointed out to me that the genitals are a delicate area; he also reminded me that all men get just one todger in their lifetime and advised me to attend the hospital for treatment.

At this point of the story, you will find similarities to that of the first story, but it gets better; in truth, for myself it gets worse.

Upon reaching the side entrance once again into the South Hants hospital in Southampton, I followed the familiar path down the long narrow corridor to the reception counter; at the reception counter, the old lady behind the counter had asked, 'Can I help you, sir?'

'Yes!' I replied, hoping that she had not recognised me from my last visit. 'I have hurt myself down below,' I remarked nervously. After I had given her all the details on how I had obtained the present injury to my manhood, the receptionist wrote down the details. Then she leaned out and over the counter, and again pointed with her pencil in the direction that I had to go. After she had explained to me how to reach the waiting-room, I walked down the familiar path of the corridor.

On reaching the swinging doors, I entered into the waiting-room to await the expected woman doctor. Looking around the waiting-room, there were the same old familiar rows of empty chairs and not a soul to be seen. As I sat down into a chair to read a magazine, I heard the familiar noise of swinging doors opening and then shutting. Looking up from the magazine, I could see coming towards myself the very same woman doctor who had treated me before. 'Mr Johnson?' she asked, holding a folder in her hand.

'Yes!' I replied, with a red face.

'Will you please follow me!' she asked, turning to enter into the small room beside the swinging doors. As she placed the folder upon the table in the small room, I wondered if she remembered me from our last meeting.

Confident that she had not remembered me, I started to take my clothes off as she said, 'Take all your clothes off, and then jump up on to the bed please.'

'Do you want me to take my socks off as well as all my clothing?' I asked knowingly.

'Yes! And the socks please,' replied the woman doctor in a soft voice.

Once again, she left the room with the same old smile as I continued to undress. I then jumped upon the bed to await her return. Whilst sitting in an upright position upon the bed, I covered my bruised baby-making machine with the small rubber sheet that I found neatly folded on the bottom end of the bed.

The woman doctor reappeared; I had not dared to ask her where the doctor was.

'Lay back upon the bed please and face the wall with your legs up,' she ordered, as she moved once again towards my injured manhood.

It was very quiet within the small room; there was not a sound to be heard as she fiddled with my love tool with silky fingers at the other end of the bed, whilst I was counting the marks upon the wall and the polyester tiles upon the ceiling to take away the pressure of my present predicament. The woman doctor seemed to be looking at my baby-making machine for hours; but in truth, it was only a minute or so.

The silence within the small room was soon broken as she uttered in a loud voice, 'I have seen this before!'

As she spoke the words that I did not want to hear, I held tight to the rubber sheeting that I was lying upon, with my fingers now showing the whites of my knuckles. I could have died there and then. I could feel my own face running red with embarrassment; it was the way that she had shouted, 'I have seen this before!' I did not know whether I had the biggest todger in the world, or the smallest.

The doctor turned to face me with a smile, as she ordered me to get off the bed and on to the floor. Six months had passed since she last saw my baby-making machine; she had not recognised me for myself; it was unbelievable. This woman doctor must have seen lots of different people within the last six months; obviously, this doctor had not read my file at the time of my examination; if she had done so, she would not have uttered those words in the manner that she had spoken them. I was now standing upon the floor behind her, naked, as she turned from a trolley that held an assortment of bandages and surgical instruments. As I stood there naked with my bruised todger dangling as if that too had died, she applied a small dressing to my manhood. After applying the tiny dressing, the doctor gave me an injection because of the rusty nail.

'That's it! You can get dressed now,' the doctor said as she put away the syringe and cotton wool. 'If you get any further trouble, go and see your GP,' she added on leaving the room.

I could not get dressed fast enough. My exit from the hospital was much faster than my entrance. I will never forget those words, 'I have seen this before.' Those words have been ringing in my ears ever since. I wonder why?

The Big Sleep

In my youth, many years ago, I had a terrible job getting up in the mornings; I was always dead to the world. Not even an exploding bomb would have awakened me from my deep slumber as I snored away the night and the best part of the day. This terrible affliction lost me many a good job in the past. My poor old mother, who has since long gone, suffered immensely with the overpowering strain upon trying to get me up and out of bed, to go to work in the mornings. Sometimes, truth can sound stranger than fiction; but this story, I can assure you, is definitely not fiction. My sleeping problem did change when I got married. My new stressed-out wife had now taken over the role of my mother. In my youth, I was very angry, fed up, and annoyed with myself over the never-ending loss of employment. Something had to be done; but what? I hadn't a clue! It was not that I was lazy, I didn't mind doing a job of work; in fact, when I was up and out of the bed, I would become a workaholic. There were evenings whereupon I would go to bed at eight, to make sure that I would be up and ready for work for the following morning; but it made no difference, I still slept through the night and a part of that following day. I dreaded the coming of each morning until finally a solution was at hand; my stressed-out wife made an appointment to see the doctor in connection with her own women's complaints; so I decided to tag along with her. The doctor's place of practice was a converted house upon the Bursledon Road in Southampton; at the doctor's, my wife and I sat within a very small room with the doctor in attendance. My wife at that time was unaware of my true intentions, and the reasons why I had accompanied her to the surgery that day. Whilst my wife was sorting out her complaints with the doctor, I sat quietly nearby within the same consulting room; as I sat there, I was trying to build up enough courage to ask the doctor if he had something that would get me up in the mornings. After the doctor had finished talking to my wife, I then nervously blurted out what I myself was really there for. The doctor looked up from his desk whilst writing upon my wife's medical file; then smiled, as he looked back down to finish his writing. My wife's face had gone quite red as she looked to me upon my nervously blurting out to the doctor what I was truly there for.

When the doctor had finished writing upon my wife's medical file, he looked back up to where I was still sitting and asked, 'Now! What were you saying?'

Breaking into a nervous cold sweat with further embarrassment, I repeated the question a little more clearly.

'I thought that's what you had asked!' the doctor replied smiling, on pushing to one side the medical file upon the desk. My wife had once again gone red in the face as the doctor stood up. The doctor then said, as he turned to an old tin workman's clothing locker, situated in one corner of the small room, 'I think that I may have just the thing for you!'

I could feel my heart pounding against the inside of my chest, as he reached to the top of the tin locker to collect a very large book. My wife and I looked at each other with red faces whilst the doctor's back was to us. I was now wondering just what was it that he had in mind for me as he took the big book down from the top of the locker. Having a very large and heavy book now within his hands, the doctor turned to face my wife and I with a smirk. As the doctor moved towards the desk, he made me feel very uncomfortable and uneasy. The very large heavy book that the doctor held within his hands looked surprisingly like Merlin the Magician's book; what was to follow was unbelievably real. I could scarcely believe my own eyes, as my wife and I watched the doctor slam down the heavy book upon the desk, for as he did so, the strangest thing happened. One would really have thought that this book really was Merlin the Magician's book. As the doctor slammed down the book upon his desk, a cloud of dust erupted from the cover. My wife and I could not believe in what we both had just witnessed. The heavy book was black in colour with gold edging upon each separate page. Upon the black covering of this wondrous unbelievable-looking book was gold embroidery; the gold embroidery shone on through the remainder of the dust with a beautiful majestic glow. I again looked to my wife just as she looked back at myself; we were now both very apprehensive as to what might follow.

On slamming down this magnificent and majestic-looking book of knowledge with the dust swirling above the cover, the doctor said, as he was about to sit back into his chair, 'Let's see, what have we here?'

On opening the black dusty cover of the big book, the doctor gave a mischievous smile as he flicked on through the brightly shining golden edges upon the pages within the majestic-looking book. He then uttered, 'Yes! We should have something here for you?'

As the doctor flicked on through the pages, I could see very old-fashioned writing upon each separate page in turn with beautiful majestic colourful markings, that exceeded the bounds of one's imagination. I again looked to my stressed-out wife who once again returned to me looks to kill; she was not a happy person.

Upon settling on a page within the big book, the doctor

then said, 'Here we are!' Picking up a pen, the doctor started to write something down upon his prescription pad from a selected page of the great book with a triumphant smile.

Tearing the prescription from the pad, the doctor smiled as he handed the prescription back over to myself from across the table. 'That should sort you out!' he said just as my wife and I stood up from the two chairs. The doctor then slammed shut the big book; on doing so, a cloud of dust once again erupted from off the book, as if it were smoke amid a bright beam of sunlight, seemingly directed purposely into the room from the window and on to the majestic-looking book, in a godly manner. My stressed-out wife and I continued to watch as the light dust settled upon his once shiny desk. The doctor laughed at this on seeing my wife and me to the door.

Before leaving, the doctor said cheerfully, 'Let me know how you get on with it.'

After thanking the doctor, my stressed-out wife and I left the surgery to go and get the prescription.

Later that afternoon, my stressed-out wife and I took a bus ride to Southampton's shopping centre. Upon reaching the town, we had then to enter a chemist shop that was situated below Bar, this being part of a mediaeval castle turned into a museum; before entering the shop, we could see through the open door that the chemist shop was quite large and very busy, and there was also not too much room to move about inside with the influx and outflow of all the people who were going about their daily business.

On entering the chemist shop, I could see to the right of myself a long counter. The counter ran the length of the whole shop. The length of the counter was approximately thirty yards, it stood four feet high and approximately three feet in width across the top of the counter. At the other end of the long counter, to the other side of the aisle, was a pharmacist's office. To the left of myself were several aisles that displayed many other commodities. After entering the chemist shop, my wife and I stopped just inside to scan the surrounding area of the whole shop. We were both very sceptical as to what the prescription might prove to be upon collection and very nervous. Passing the prescription to my stressed-out wife, I told her to go down to the other end of the counter and get it filled. My stressed-out wife put up an argument; her argument was that she was not going to hand in the prescription, as she had not forgotten what had happened within the doctor's examination room; but as it was, I won the argument. As my stressed-out wife slowly and reluctantly walked on down the side of the very long counter towards the pharmacist's office, I moved to the side of the counter that was situated just inside the chemist shop's entrance to the right of myself. As I leaned upon the counter, I watched my stressed-out wife's continued reluctance as she slowly moved on down towards the pharmacist's office, whilst I myself was looking upon an array of displays that portrayed many different commodities upon the counter before myself. Holding tight within her hand the prescription, my stressed-out wife had now joined a small queue beside the counter.

Finally, ten minutes later, I could see that my wife had handed over the prescription to a young girl assistant. The young assistant had then taken the prescription back into the pharmacist's office, she in turn handed it over to the pharmacist. Having windows all around their pharmacist's office gave them a clear view of what was going on outside. The windows also enabled myself to see the young assistant talking to a male pharmacist. The pharmacist was looking at the prescription with uncertainty. The youngest pharmacist then turned to show the prescription to a senior colleague. All three were now stood looking at the prescription whilst the queue behind my wife began to grow. Slowly, I moved on down the side of the counter, I was now curious to know what was going on. On reaching the half-way mark along the counter, I stopped to observe the situation; I could see from my new stationary position approximately eight young girl assistants in white coats, who were each attending their own section of the counter serving the public. Looking back into the windows of the office from my present position, I could see the two pharmacists and the young girl assistant stepping back out of their office, and then into the aisle behind the counter to where all the other young girls were in a line along the aisle busy serving the public. Now even more curious, I moved a little further forward under the pretence that it was all nothing to do with myself; hearing a commotion with the sound of fallen bottles clinking up against one another I slowly moved down alongside the counter, I stopped once again to view the situation. I could see that the two male pharmacists and the young girl assistant were now taking bottles of all shapes and sizes from under the counter. The older pharmacist seemed to know just what he was looking for, whilst the other pharmacists and the young girl assistant had a look of uncertainty about themselves. As the older pharmacist looked on the shelving beneath the counter, he ordered the other serving girls in the aisle to stop what they were doing and to help find what the prescription demanded. Bottles of all descriptions were being taken from under the long wide counter shelving, then placed within the walkway of the aisle under their own feet. More and more bottles were strewn along the serving side of the aisle, thus making the aisle now almost impossible to walk upon. The total length of the shelving being searched was approximately nine yards from the pharmacist's office. There were three separate long shelves beneath the counter that held untold amounts of medicine bottles; there were signs of anxiety upon the faces of the staff as they searched intensively amongst the bottles for the required prescription; between them, they almost cleared the nine-yard section of shelving under the counter. As the staff continued to search in vain for the required prescription, bottles were being knocked over underfoot.

The public were now getting very agitated and curious as to what was going on. The aisle was now completely covered with an assortment of bottles, many of which were broken in the search. Having an array of bottles across the narrow aisle flooring made it very difficult for all the other serving girls to help locate the prescription with safety, whilst at the same time trying to attend to the waiting, anxious public. On moving a little nearer to the commotion, I could see that the older pharmacist was now in a very bad mood. I once again re-stationed myself approximately five yards from the pharmacist's office on reaching the end of the queue by quietly working my way down towards their end of the counter. My stressed-out wife, who was still at the head of the queue, was looking very embarrassed and displayed a deep red colour upon her face that I could see at a distance.

Moving myself a little further along the counter, midway down the queue, I entered a gap between the people standing and waiting to be served. Leaning over the counter, I could see the mess within the aisle; finally, from the back of a lower shelving, the younger pharmacist found what they were all looking for. Amongst all the commotion and the clinking of bottles, the search was called to a stop by the older pharmacist. The bottles were then handed over to the older pharmacist with a sigh of relief. Whilst leaning over the counter, I could see two bottles being held within the older pharmacist's hands. The pharmacist looked straight at me as I stood opposite him at the counter. As I looked down upon the empty surface of the counter so's not to look into his angry eyes, the pharmacist slammed down hard both jars upon the counter top just before myself. The bottle jars were brown in colour and approximately six inches in height, with a circumference of three inches around the waist; the necks were very short with broad shoulders. As I silently looked down upon the jars that were now in front of myself, I could once again not believe my own eyes; the shoulders upon each of the two jars were very much in the same condition as the big black book within the doctor's surgery; they were covered in dust. It was incredible, and yet the chemist shop had looked very clean; it was as if I were in a dream, everything that had happened that day was not real; the book, and now the dust upon the bottles; but there it was, standing straight in front of myself upon the counter. As the pharmacist slammed the bottles down upon the counter top, he said, 'There you are! You will have to come back, there are another three to come.'

I then looked up to see to whom he was talking to. I then realised, that it was I whom he was addressing; how on earth could he have known it was for me? I will never know.

My stressed-out wife had now moved from the front of the queue to be by my side. People waiting within the queue were looking at us both with looks of intimidation. Feeling now very embarrassed and red in the face, I picked up the two brown jars, then moved away from the counter. Just as I had done so, the staff behind the counter started to replace all the other bottles on the shelves. I looked to see where my wife was as I turned to leave the counter; she had quietly disappeared from sight. Upon leaving the counter, the customers gave to me the most foul glare of disapproval; I could not leave the chemist shop quick enough. On leaving the counter for the exit, I could still hear the clinking sounds of bottles behind myself being re-stacked on the shelves, which was followed by the moans and groans of the stressed-out staff. Once outside the chemist shop, I felt a sense of relief. I found my stressed-out wife further down the road looking into the window of another shop. I did not get any peace from her all the way home.

Upon reaching our home, I took one of the jars from out of a carrier bag. The jar still had traces of dust around the broad shoulders at the base of the bottles' necks. On opening one of the brown jars, my eyes widened as I looked at the contents within the jar; inside the jar were very large pills that were similar in shape to a liquorice comfort sweet, but three times thicker. The size of these pills looked like they had been made for the treatment of a horse. They were huge. The instructions read, *Take one at night before going to bed, then one three times a day*. I tried those oversize pills for two weeks, and at first, they seemed to work for me. But after the two weeks, they had no more effect; I was once again back into my oversleeping mode.

Three weeks later, I gave the two jars of pills intact to one of my brothers; for he too had the very same problem as I, he could not get up in the mornings for work. Nearly three months later, that very same brother returned back to my home and asked if I had any more of the pills left over, for he used up all the pills that I had previously given to him. I then told him that I had given him all the pills that I had; but, if he was to go back to the chemist shop in town, there should be three more bottles awaiting my collection. I then, out of curiosity, asked my brother, 'Did those other pills work for you?'

He replied, 'Well no! They did not get me up in the mornings, but they sure as hell made me randy.'

The Dream

Some years ago I was in a very deep sleep in my bed on one very cold winter's night. Sleeping alongside my wife kept me nice and warm, and very snug and comfortable in the very cold winter months. Winter and summer, I always slept with nothing on. So the colder it was, the closer I snuggled into my wife. Upon this particular cold winter's night, I was snuggled up very close to my wife in the deepest of sleep. Whilst I was sleeping, a dream materialised within my head. I dreamt that I was in prison, cleaning the prison's enormous toilets. From wall to wall, floor to ceiling, was covered in white tiles. Whilst I was having this dream, I knew at the back of my mind that I had an urgent need to get out of bed, to have a piss; but I was too snug and warm to move. Back in my dream, I was for some unknown reason sweeping water upon the white tiled floor into the men's urinal drain. The strangest thing of all, I was sweeping the white tiled floor with a road sweeper's very big stiff brush; as I was sweeping over the white tiles with this enormous brush, in stepped another prisoner to have a piss into the urinal drain.

I looked at him and said, 'If anyone wants me, I am just going for a wee.'

The other prisoner replied, 'Okay!'

After throwing down the brush on the wet tiled floor, I walked towards another door that led on into another room. The room that I was now in, was very much the same as the room that I had just left, but with a difference.

This room had the very same white tiles from wall to wall, floor to ceiling with an additional set of toilets. Whilst still dreaming, I was squirming in my sleep to force out the need to go and have a piss. In my dream, whilst standing within this tiled room, I could see to the front of myself ten cubicles. The cubicles had no doors on them. At a distance of two yards, I could see that all the toilet pans had no seats upon them. The toilet pans themselves were covered inside and out with excretion; there seemed to have been an epidemic of diarrhoea throughout the prison. On looking at the very wet and runny diarrhoea plastered all over the toilet pans, inside and out, and all over the floor, I said to myself, 'I'm not going in there.' Stepping backwards about three feet on what appeared to be sawdust, I further said to myself, 'That's it! I can't wait any longer, I will have to go here.' Taking out my baby-making machine, I started to let go the heavily over-stored urine. As I let go of the urine, I felt a sense of relief; but suddenly I awoke from my dream in a flash! Looking down between my wife and myself with the help of the moonlight shining on through the window, I immediately noticed, that I had in fact pissed all up my wife's back! My wife, who at the time was wearing a night-dress, was completely soaked through to the skin, and stayed unbelievably fast asleep throughout my ordeal. I placed the flat of my hand on the back of her soaked night-dress, only to flick off my hand enough dripping urine to fill an egg cup. My wife and the bed were completely saturated by a torrent of urine. Pushing the wet sheets from under myself towards her already waterlogged back, I then decided to finish off my piss in the bathroom. The bath-room was exactly what it was called, there was no toilet pan. Hanging my baby-making machine over the bath, I let loose the remainder of the urine that was still swelled up inside myself into the bath. On my return to the bedroom, I wrapped a dry part of the bed covering that was on my side of the bed, back around my body and on to the wet mattress, then went back into a deep, warm, snug, but damp, sleep. In the morning, my wife did not utter a word on what had happened that night. Later that day, my wife and I went to visit a friend around the corner from where we lived.

As we both sat there talking to my friend and his wife, I said, 'Did I tell you about my dream?'

My wife who was oblivious to what I was going to say, looked up and said, 'What dream?'

I then told my friend and his wife what I had dreamt.

After I had finished telling them all about my dream, my stressed-out wife looked up and said with embarrassment, 'You bastard! I thought that was where you had been sweating all night!'

She didn't speak to me for two days after that. She wasn't a happy person.

The Wasps' Nest

In 1993 I witnessed the strangest thing that one could possibly imagine. It was widely known by the media that England had been invaded by killer wasps. The public were warned not to tamper with a nest if any member of the public found one, and to get in touch with a professional person to remove or destroy such a find.

Upon one very hot summer's day, I had to remove from an old barn two thousand condemned bales of straw. The barn at that time had no roof to keep the straw dry; consequently, all the bales had gotten very wet and decayed. Whilst removing some of the condemned bales of straw, I noticed a few wasps flying around the inside of the barn. First off, I was not taking too much notice of them, even though a few of them were flying about my head. Upon the second day, whilst I was removing some more of the condemned bales, I started to notice that there were more wasps then usual flying around a wide area within the barn and about my head. My son and I, in the course of our work, had pulled back from off the heap a bale of straw. On removing the bale of straw, we had to let it fall to the ground and run like the blazes to the field outside. Looking back into the barn from a safe distance, we could see an increase in the wasps, as they flew above the area to where the bale was last removed. My son and I were surprised to see that we had unearthed from beneath the old bale of straw a round wasp nest, about the size of a small football. On seeing the nest, my son threw a large lump of wood at it, destroying it completely. The wasps were not too happy about their nest being broken up, so we had to leave what we were doing for another day.

Two days later my cousin arrived just as my son and I had started to remove some more of the condemned bales. My cousin noticed there were a few wasps flying about the field and around the barn area upon his entry to the farm. My son told him about the nest that we had unearthed and destroyed previously. Later that day, after loading up more of the wet bales, which were falling apart and quite black with mould, on to a transit pick-up truck; we noticed that the amount of wasps flying around had increased once again. On pulling some more of the bales down from the heap, we noticed that the wasps were now flying in a concentrated area to where we were now working. Leaving the wasps to disperse, we decided to off-load what we had already loaded on the truck to the rear of the field. On our return to the roofless barn with an empty truck for another load, we could see that the wasps had not dispersed, but had increased in size to an unacceptable number. The three of us stood back looking at the wasps that flew about our work area. Picking up a long metal pole, I braved the wasps as I stepped back into the open barn. On entering the barn, I pushed over two or three soggy bales of straw together, from the top of the stack. As the bails fell to the ground, the wasps became a mass above the heap. Knocking to the ground one more soggy bale with a long pole, we could not believe our eyes as to what we were now looking at. The last falling bale had revealed a huge wasps' nest; one and a half times bigger than a football. The wasps had gone a little mental upon the uncovering of their nest. The wasps very quickly converged into a dark cloud above the unbroken nest that was clearly visible between the next two bales on the top of the heap; on momentarily seeing this dark mass above the nest, I looked to my son and my cousin and said,

'Run!'

My cousin stayed frozen upon the spot as my son and I gave distance. My cousin, who was looking directly up at the dark mass, that was obviously about to strike, stood in amazement at the sight before him. The dark mass decided to make their move. As one, they had passed my cousin, who had not moved, and gone directly for the sheep dog that was behind my cousin looking into the barn from the outside. The black and white sheep dog immediately became one mass of black and yellow in colour. My son ran to the yelping dog to beat the wasps from off her with his bare hands. Momentarily, after beating most of the wasps from off the dog, we all ran for cover into a Portacabin that was situated nearby; looking out of the window, the sky outside was now full of bad-tempered flying wasps; they were everywhere. Two hours later, the wasps flying about the sky had thinned out considerably. Braving it, we all ventured back out into the open field. After walking slowly and cautiously back to the barn, we all stood for a moment looking at the size of the nest with disbelief; the three of us then started to throw objects at the large white ball in order to destroy it. The nest broke into two pieces upon contact with the missiles. Half the nest fell down to the ground, whilst the other half stayed firmly fixed upon the straw stack. On our breaking the nest in two, a considerable amount of wasps descended from nowhere and everywhere, and then on down towards the broken half, that had situated itself upon the ground, whilst wasps reappeared about our heads. On seeing the wasps starting to grow in numbers, we all made a second dash back into the Portacabin, followed by the dog for further protection; we could see that the wasps were very angry. The dog was none the worse for her experience with the yellow coat that she was wearing earlier; she was being extra-cautious towards the wasps with a high degree of respect for their strength in numbers.

Night time was now upon us, and my cousin had gone home. When it was dark, I went back out to the barn with torch in hand; in the barn, I poured one gallon of used black sump oil all over the half-broken wasp's nest that lay upon the ground. The next day, I could see that I had killed quite a lot of the wasps; but there still were lots more, hovering over the broken half upon the ground, even though the half nest was drenched in oil. In view of the amount still hovering above the half nest, late that same night, I again poured black sump oil over the same half wasps' nest upon the ground to ensure their destruction.

The following day, I looked back into the barn at the half-broken nest that was saturated in the black sump oil; there was a huge number of wasps now lying dead. A few wasps were flying about the barn, but the threat of retaliation was now gone; At least, I thought it was.

Early next morning, my son and I again returned to the barn to have another look at the half wasps' nest that was saturated in oil; as we stood looking down at the half nest upon the floor amid a large puddle of sump oil, we both heard a sound that sounded like a queen bee in flight. Both my son and I looked upwards towards the other half of the nest that was still situated upon the straw stack and free from the oil; we both stood there with open mouths as we witnessed a sight that was in appearance unnatural and unbelievable; we could not believe what we were now seeing. For coming out of the other half of the wasps' nest were three enormous wasps. The size of these wasps in comparison to a queen bee was also unbelievable; they were, in our view, slightly bigger then a queen bee. The three giant wasps flew down towards the other dead wasps that were floating within the black sump oil upon the ground; the sound of their wings in flight was very frightening. These giant wasps reminded me of Sumo wrestlers, with their bulk weight slowly moving in flight. We both watched these giants hovering very close over their dead in the sump oil. It appeared to us that they had come out from the other half of the nest to look and see where their army had gotten too. Looking again at the Sumos, as I had nicknamed them, doesn't even come into the scope of one's imagination; they were unbelievable, they were something out of a film. My son and I were now wondering if these Sumo type wasps were some sort of special guard for the queen; that is, if there was a queen still within the other half of the broken nest. I then said to my son that there must be at least two more of those Sumos left within the other half of the nest, to guard the queen, as I could not see her being left unprotected. Looking at these very large unusual wasps was very frightening; I have never seen anything like it before. What we both witnessed, may not have been recorded or seen before by any other person; we could have been the very first to have witnessed such an event; or maybe it has been already recorded elsewhere; or possibly, the whole story about these Sumos has been kept under wraps; who knows? My son and I moved away from the barn very quickly for our own safety.

In the late afternoon, we both returned to the barn with a little bit more respect for what was in there. Upon a further inspection of the nest, we could both see no sign of the Sumos or any other living wasps; only the dead floating upon the black sump oil, that had spread across the ground over a wide area. The broken half of the wasps' nest upon the straw stack was now totally empty.

The Secret Assignment

Some years ago, in and around the Sixties, I had to collect a five-yard tipper lorry from a Portsmouth naval base. When I got there, I found that the tipper lorry that I was to collect was already fully loaded and ready to roll. This tipper lorry had a top fly sheet covering the consignment load, so I hadn't a clue what I was carrying. The paperwork for the consignment load was sealed, and the only paperwork that I was allowed to have was the actual delivery address in Southampton. Upon driving back to Southampton, I found the roads to have been unusually clear in regard to the amount of traffic that was normally upon the road on that day. The load within the rear of the lorry seemed rather heavy. My destination for the off-loading was inside another naval base in the Netley, Southampton area. Today, that naval base is no longer there; they have since built houses for the public upon the grounds which in later years caused a storm because of the toxic waste that had been found dumped beneath the ground.

Upon my arrival at the Netley naval base with my un-known cargo, I was met at the gate by a naval security officer; the naval security officer took from me the sealed papers, and then directed me further into the base.

I had not driven ten yards, when I was again stopped by another security officer. Stopping me in the middle of the road, he further directed me in yet another direction. My new direction led me into a dead end; thereupon, another naval person said to me, 'Take off the top fly sheet, then reverse back upon this crusher.'

I looked at the rather large crushing machine that looked very much like the rear of a dust cart without wheels, then to the fly sheet above the lorry. Climbing up between the cab of the lorry and the rear tipping box, I reached the fly sheet covering that had to be removed from off the top rear of the lorry. Pulling back one corner of the fly cover sheet, I peeked inside to see what my load was; I had the shock of my life when my eyes fell upon the cargo inside. For there in front of myself, was an array of small fire arms, machine guns, and an assortment of knives with bayonets, neatly fitted between each other running flush and level, to the very top of the lorry. I now know why the load that I was carrying was extra heavy. I was not a happy person.

After completely removing the top fly sheet, then climbing back down from the rear of the lorry, I asked the naval person working the press, 'What's all this then?'

The naval person replied, 'They are now obsolete and have to be crushed up in the press.'

'What's wrong with them?' I asked curiously.

'Nothing,' replied the naval person, 'they have been replaced with new ones,' he added, as he stood by the driving door upon my lorry. The naval person then moved to one side as I backed up on to the crusher.

After tipping the consignment up into the crusher, I said to the naval person, 'This is all wrong, my life has been put in jeopardy carrying this lot!'

'What do you mean?' asked the naval person.

'I could have been stopped by the IRA, that's what I mean,' I replied in annoyance.

'No! You had no fear of that!' replied the naval person. 'I can assure you you weren't alone!' he added with a confident smile.

Upon my journey from Portsmouth to Southampton, I had not seen any other vehicle following me whilst en route. I often think about the secret assignment that was given to me without my knowledge and permission in the Sixties; one never knows just what one is carrying from time to time, apparently! I was told later that it was one of the safest ways for the government to move materials about without drawing attention to themselves; what about the poor driver, I say. As the driver, I did not get anything extra for doing the job. All a driver will get from an underhanded assignment secretly placed upon him without his knowledge, will possibly be insurance cover for loss of life.

Again in the Sixties, one of my brothers rolled backwards down a hill with an unknown assignment. The type of vehicle that he was driving at that time was an articulated lorry; the brakes upon the articulated lorry failed to work. The articulated lorry was carrying a very large freighter box upon the rear of its trailer.

The trailer and freighter box to the rear of the cab had landed up balancing over a railway line from off a bridge like a see-saw after first running through a brick wall. My brother was like myself; he was not a happy person.

The vehicle was surrounded by many police officers within a very short time of his accident. They were everywhere. The roads were completely blocked off, one could see nothing but police. After the trailer with its freighter box still intact was pulled out and away from its balancing position to safety, it was then towed away by a very large tow truck, accompanied by police. At the scene of the accident, not one police officer approached my brother to ask him what happened.

As time passed, it was forgotten about. The incident died a quiet death. The haulage contractor whom my brother was driving for was also never approached by the authorities over the accident; it was all very hush-hush! My brother, unlike myself, hadn't a clue to this day, what he was carrying. If asked, the government would no doubt make a full denial of all such contracts that were undertaken by unsuspecting hauliers. The secrecy over those assignments must still go on today.

The Lost Hour

In the Sixties, I worked as a binman on the city of South-ampton corporation dust-carts. On different occasions, I and my three brothers worked together upon the same dust-cart. There were in those days, seven binmen to a gang upon each round; each round had their own area for the emptying of the dustbins from houses and sometimes schools and shops. Each separate round also had two lorries to take away all the rubbish for disposal to a local tip, or incinerator. As binmen, we had an elaborate title befitting a king. The elaborate title that was ordained upon us all in those days was that of a Refuse Disposal Officer. Yes sir! That was a grand title for an ordinary binman in those days.

If all the rounds throughout Southampton had a full gang with no person off sick, then this would leave the spare binmen who were kept in reserve, stationed within the yard of the depot. The depot was situated in the Corporation Wharf, Albert Road, Southampton. The Corporation Wharf was where the big silver lorries off-loaded their rubbish into an incinerator, and sometimes the smaller side shutter lorries from off the rounds, if they were not too far away from the depot. The smaller side shutter lorries upon each round had on tow to the rear a large box trailer. The box trailer was for putting all the old waste paper and cardboard into, this was useful salvage for recycling. The waste paper and cardboard was then thrown into a big shed from the trailers within the Corporation Wharf upon entering the yard. The waste paper and the cardboard were then separated. After separating the two, both the cardboard and newspapers were placed into an old press for baling. The very slow outdated hand-baling machine was operated by an older yard hand due for retirement. Because there was only the one old hand press for baling, the waste paper and cardboard waiting to be baled had accumulated into a rather large mountain within a very large shed. The accumulation of waste heightened to approximately thirty feet, with a base circumference of twenty-five feet; the mountain of waste paper situated almost from the entrance of the shed to the rear of the shed. The recycling shed was very heavily infested by very large rats; a strong musty odour emitted itself from within the old shed to the yard outside. Because the old baling machine could not keep up with the demand upon the never-ending daily loads, that entered the shed each day, half the mountain of cardboard and paper buried under the daily loads had been there for years. This big recycling shed was also where all the spare binmen would spend their time. The spare binmen would all wait within the shed daily, so that they could be called upon at any time as a replacement for any shortages of manpower that might occur upon a round. It did not matter if a spare man was late upon arrival to the large shed in the mornings, as there was nothing for him to do but wait. There have been times when five or more spare binmen would wait daily within the large shed for a week or more; having nothing to do whilst waiting to be called out on a round, the spare binmen would mess about all day within the shed having fun to pass the time. Upon arrival at the big shed in the mornings, there was no need to clock on for a day's pay; when they were short of manpower upon a round, and a spare binman was called out from the big shed to make up their numbers, his name would be placed into a book by the driver or charge-hand at the start of each day; this was then sent back into the pay office each week to let them know that the spare man selected from the shed, had been put out upon a round. Waiting within the large shed all day long could get very boring. Every spare binman who turned in for the day was always half an hour late for duty. Being late was no big deal as a spare binman, as it has always been that way; no person in the office was worried about it, as long as all the men turned in for stand-by. I personally was very happy with this arrangement, for I had a terrible job getting out of bed in the mornings; as we all know from my other stories within this book. But the good life, after many years of being allowed to start work at eight thirty instead of eight o'clock, with pay, suddenly came to an unexpected halt. A newcomer was about to deliberately change the system to suit himself, from what we as spare binmen had become accustomed to over the years. The company had taken off from the road maintenance crew a foreman who was also due to retire within the next two weeks. This foreman was placed in the recycling shed from the road repair team, to see out the remainder of his last few days before retirement. He was not expected by the company to do any kind of work whatsoever within those last few days.

Upon the arrival of this retiring foreman I and five other spare binmen were trying to catch the large rats that were breeding in abundance within the very old waste paper and cardboard. The retiring foreman did not say too much upon his arrival in the shed, he just stood there watching, and assessing what we were all doing; in truth, he had no power over us, or any other person. He was now only there for the passing of time. The retiring foreman was approximately five feet seven in height, hard-faced, grumpy, and very fat; upon his arrival, he just stood at the entrance of the shed, looking back in at us with his hands neatly placed into the side pockets of his new blue overalls; whilst we, the spare binmen, were all jumping about the sloping sides of the paper mountain trying to catch the rats. He watched us with contempt as we continued to jump from one place to another, stamping upon any old piece of surface paper or cardboard that had been slightly moved underfoot by the scavenging rats that were tunnelling and foraging beneath; sometimes we were successful; rats would be caught underfoot and killed by jumping on the cardboard as it moved by flattening them; it was all great fun, and passed the time of day. For the next two days, the retiring foreman just stood and watched what we were all doing; he was not the sort of person to strike up a conversation, he had this silly habit of writing to himself silly little notes within his note book; it looked as if he were assessing the work situation, plus every person within the big shed and around the whole surrounding complex.

Upon the third day, I arrived at the shed in readiness for a possible call-out at eight thirty as normal. Officially, it was an eight o'clock start, but who cared? As long as I was there. On my arrival to the big shed with my push-bike, I found the retiring foreman waiting at the entrance. He stood proudly with a note book in one hand, and a pencil held high within the other. Upon my seeing him now standing before me as I was about to enter the shed, he blocked my way into the shed with his person and said, 'Name?'

I looked at him with dismay and wonder. Uncertain to his motive, I answered, 'What!'

He again repeated whilst holding pen to paper, 'Name?'

I looked at him in bewilderment as I asked, 'What do you want my name for?'

'Because you're late!' he replied in a loud stern voice.

This retiring foreman had taken it upon himself to be in charge of the waste shed without the proper authority of the council office; he had, in fact, ordained himself to be in total command. Reluctantly, I gave him my name just as the others had done upon their arrival.

The following morning, upon my arrival at the big shed, the self-appointed retiring foreman was again waiting for my arrival, and again said upon confrontation, 'Name?'

On dismounting my push-bike, I replied, 'What! Again? You already have my name.'

'You're late! Name?' he asked again with a strong voice of authority.

I looked at his hard but sincere face as I shouted, 'I am not going to keep repeating myself every time I see you! If you don't like that as an answer, then go and see them in the office; and whilst we are at it, who the hell do you think you are? You are a nobody, just an old fool waiting for retirement with nothing better to do.'

The retiring foreman just stood and looked at me for a moment, then turned to sit down upon a chair that was situated just inside the entrance to the shed; as he had done so, he started to put pen to paper.

Upon that same day, I was standing within the shed just out of earshot of the retiring foreman, talking to the other spare binmen about him; I told the other spare hands that come tomorrow morning, I was going to get here early before the retiring foreman. I would then be waiting for him with a note book and pencil. The other spare binmen laughed at the idea as they saw the funny side of what was to come. 'I mean it, I'm not joking,' I added as they were still laughing. The foreman looked on with suspicion as to what we were laughing about.

The next morning, surprisingly, I was up bright and early with the help of my stressed-out wife; I left home for work at ten to seven in the morning for an eight o'clock start. Going by the radio, the alarm clock, and my stressed-out wife, I should be one hour early on reaching my place of work upon leaving home. The journey to work normally took ten minutes by push-bike; but by peddling madly downhill all the way, I reached the main gate to my works at approximately two minutes to seven.

On reaching the main gate of the Corporation yard in record time, I decided that as I was so early, I would have some fun catching the rats in the shed, whilst waiting to catch the retiring foreman with my note book and pencil. After parking up my push-bike, I then walked towards the big waste shed. On reaching the shed, I stopped in my tracks at the entrance; I was utterly gobsmacked. Standing there before myself was the retiring foreman. 'Name?' he asked in a loud superior deep-sounding voice.

'What do you mean, name?' I asked with confusion.

'You're late!' he replied in a sarcastic voice.

'Late! What do you mean late?' I asked, laughing into his face.

'You are late, and I want your name and pay number please,' he replied whilst licking the end of his pencil and holding ready the note book.

'All right! You have had your joke,' I remarked as I was about to pass by him to enter on into the big shed.

'I'm not joking,' he replied whilst once again blocking my way into the shed with his person.

Again I laughed at him, as I tried to pass him by.

'Take a good look at the clock upon the wall!' he added, pointing into the direction of the big factory clock with his pencil.

With a smile, I looked up at the big clock that was situated high up upon another building, further down the yard from the entrance to the shed. The smile upon my own face widened as I turned to face the clock; for I knew only too well that it was impossible for me to have been late. The smile on my face faded as I looked at the time on the big clock.

'That's wrong!' I shouted.

'It's right!' he snapped.

I was not a happy person. I turned to look at the other

spare binmen who had themselves arrived early to see the retiring foreman being confronted by myself with note book and pencil in hand. Bewildered, and now unsure as to the truth, I asked the other binmen, 'What is the right time?'

'It's five past eight!' answered one of the spare binmen.

I was then lost for words.

'Name!' shouted the retiring foreman with a smirk whilst holding the lead of his pencil to the page of his note book.

Somehow, somewhere, I had lost an hour of my life upon that journey downhill to work; an hour of my life that I could not account for; it was mind-boggling. That lost hour has haunted me to this day, many years later. I never did find out where I had lost that hour.

The Unidentified
Flying Objects

In 1978, on a Boxing Day, five of my children aged fourteen months, seven years, nine years, thirteen years and
fourteen years, plus my wife who was then thirty-seven, all
witnessed a UFO sighting upon the dark evening of Boxing
Day at 7 p.m.

My wife and children had just left my wife's mother's
home situated upon the corner of Daffodil Road,
Swaythling in Southampton when this strange unexpected
phenomenon took place. My wife and family left my wife's
mother's home to catch the number six bus back to our
own home in the Shirley Warren area of Southampton. The
journey by bus to our home from her mother's home was
approximately seven miles. The bus-stop for that journey
was about a half hour's walk from my wife's mother's
home. Unlike today, there was only one bus on service
every hour to the public over the Christmas period. On
turning left into Carnation Road from her mother's home
upon the pavement, they all walked approximately four
yards further along the road before coming to a sudden
stop. The reason for stopping so abruptly was that they had
all heard a very loud high-pitched noise above their heads.
The noise that they were hearing was so loud that it hurt
their ears. Whilst holding their hands over their ears to
block out the ear-splitting sound, my oldest son, upon
hearing the noise, looked up to where he thought the noise

was coming from. My oldest son was the first to sight a very large object above them. My wife confirmed that the object was approximately thirty yards ahead of themselves, and was hovering just a few feet above a lamppost situated upon the same pavement, towards their bus-stop.

My oldest son's own documented account of what he saw was that the very large object hovering above the lamppost immediately glided towards the houses upon the opposite side of the road. Upon hearing the same noise, my wife and the other four children all looked up momentarily, after my oldest son first sighted the object above themselves. The object had slowly drifted across the road from the lamppost, to the opposite side of the road towards the roof-tops of the houses, my wife and children watched in disbelief as it then stopped two feet above the chimney pots hovering. Taking their hands away from their ears as the loud noise softened a little, they all stood in astonishment upon the pavement.

My wife's own documented account to what she witnessed – upon her first sighting of the floating object was that she could not understand what it was that she was actually looking at, even though the object was well lit up, and figures could be clearly seen within the strange craft. On seeing what was now without a doubt a space craft, they all covered their ears once again with their hands, as the noise that was being emitted from the strange craft had once again become very deafening. All six of my family were now looking straight at the space craft! Together they froze upon the pavement with fear and disbelief. By their own agreed account, the space craft was twice the size of a house. They then stated that the craft looked rather menacing as it lingered above the chimney pots in an almost motionless position. They were all unsure as to what the space craft's true intentions were. Together my family stood watching in amazement and feared for their own safety. My wife and oldest son then stated that the craft was completely stationary for a few seconds before starting to bounce slightly up and down, giving the appearance that it was being held up by an invisible and very strong elastic of a sort.

A further description given by three members of my family was that the craft had lights illuminating a spectrum of colours all around its outer shell; colours unknown to earthly beings such as ourselves. Because of the illuminating lights that surrounded the outside edge of the space craft, the shape of the craft could be seen to be similar to that of a spinning top, but a little flatter within its centre. They also stated that there was one single light, red in colour, flickering as it ran all around the outer edge of the craft. Upon the underbelly of the craft, there were smaller lights encircling its centre. My wife and sons then stated there were wide sloping slit-type windows running all around the upper half of the craft. The centre slit window upon the craft was much wider in appearance to the others. My wife and sons further stated that within the centre slit, three figures could plainly be seen by all. The figures within the craft were of feminine features, male, Caucasians. All three figures were dressed in white. Two members of my family stated the three figures that were clearly in view had very little hair; the small amount of hair that they had was swept back over the head from front to back. The colour of their hair looked very fair within the well-lit control room of the craft. It was also stated by two members of my family that they had rather large foreheads. Three of my family stated two figures within sat looking out, doing something with their hands. The third figure was, in appearance, standing and supervising. Four members of my family then stated the windows where the figures could plainly be seen were a blaze of bright white lights; the bright lights gave a clear view of what else my wife and children could see within the space craft. Two of my family stated that behind the figures was a centre structure that was in appearance, round in shape, running from the ceiling to floor; it appeared to be some sort of column. Because it was a very dark evening, the colour of the actual craft could not be ascertained, in respect of the spectrum of unearthly lights that seemed to be all around the craft. As all my family stood and watched this strange phenomenon, they all then witnessed the following unexpected movement of this strange craft. The space craft started once again to bounce up and down slightly before moving off very slowly, parallel to the roof-tops. The craft was now skimming the roof-tops, whilst moving slowly along the line of houses into the same direction that my family was to take for the number six bus. Approximately thirty yards further along, the space craft stopped again. Then suddenly without warning, the craft moved off at a great speed that is not possible by our standards. As it moved off at a great speed, the craft gave out a very loud sound upon an immediate right turn, then disappeared out of sight.

As the craft zoomed off, lots of people came running out of their homes to see what the loud noise was about. But it was too late, they had all missed it. The first sighting of this craft, up to its departure, lasted but only a few seconds. As we all know, a few seconds can seem like a few minutes, and then a few minutes an hour. Time has its own way of slowing things. One can often see and hear rather a lot more then one can imagine when in appearance time itself stands still. Boxing Day in those days was an empty day, and very quiet. Sunday in those days was very much like Boxing Day; it was a quiet day and very respected. If one was to see a push-bike upon a Sunday, or Christmas week, then one would be very lucky to have done so. As for the space craft hovering above the roof-tops, it gave my family the appearance that it was observing; but observing what? There was nothing to observe, the roads were empty of life, except for my own wife and children. What was to follow this strange sighting on my family's return home was very frustrating for them all.

Upon their return home, they all at the same time tried to tell me what they had just seen. I had to make them all stop talking, before I myself was able to listen to each one in turn. After they had all explained to me upon what they had seen, I then gave to each member of my family, a piece of paper and a pencil; I then told them all to go into a different part of the house, and draw exactly what each of them had seen. When they had all drawn what they had seen, I then called them all together. The drawings of the space craft were almost identical. It was very uncanny. Without a doubt, the drawings clearly prove that they all had seen something very similar; but what they had seen could have been something entirely different to what it really was. I personally have always kept an open mind after that incident; after all, if there is life here, then why not elsewhere. My oldest son, who is now thirty-two years of age, said to me, 'When one has seen a UFO, one is always looking to the sky.' The sighting that my family witnessed at that time, was never reported. The reason for not reporting what they had all witnessed, was simply because of the many crackpots who say they have seen UFOs; but in truth, have not. It's the crackpots who make other people's true stories, just like my own family's, very unbelievable to others.

As the years passed, my family still talk about that day in 1978. I never ever thought that I would ever see a UFO in my own lifetime. But then it happened! Now because of what I personally saw, I now know that my family saw what they claimed to have seen.

As strange as it may sound, destiny sometimes plays a

major part within one's life. One cannot always foretell the future. Most of the population in the world has never seen a UFO, whilst others see them without even trying. Sometimes, only one person at a time will witness such an event. And there are times when two or three will have a sighting together; there are also complete families who have witnessed such an unexpected strange phenomenon together. I can now include my own family as well as myself to that list. My own first sighting was years apart from that of my own family. Some people may say that families like my own are of a chosen few by the aliens, to be able to see such a phenomenon. That is utter rubbish; it is but a chance in life; being there at the right time, and looking up at the right time. How often does one really look up? Not very often. Because one does not always look up, one might miss one's only chance in a lifetime to witness such an event. This now brings me to my own personal sighting many years after my own family's sighting. My own sighting was also a chance in life; I now feel very honoured to have witnessed such an event.

In the month of June 1995, my oldest son and I witnessed another UFO sighting. My oldest son and I were at the time of the sighting working for Bowmer and Kirkland Limited, upon the Lower Link Farm, St Mary Bourne, Andover. We both were working upon the building of a new factory that was being built for Vita Cress. My own very first sighting of a UFO was at seven thirty in the morning as I was driving to work with my oldest son. The morning was getting very hot, and the sky was very clear and very blue. There was not a cloud to be seen. It was one of those odd days when the sun was at its fullest, and looked very close to the earth. The size of the sun at that time looked like another giant planet about to collide with the earth, it was of a colossal size. The sun was to the right of myself, whilst I was driving into work along a country lane. The moon was much the same as the sun; it was at its fullest and almost as colossal. The sun was as bright as it could ever have gotten. The moon was almost as bright as the sun. The moon was upon the left of my person and to the rear of my car as I was driving along. Having both the sun and the moon up at the same time was in itself a rarity. One does not very often see a day like that, and with such magnificence. That day was full of grandeur, and had a breathtaking view of its own as we drove on down the country road. As my son and I drove down the country road, we could see a small humpback bridge ahead of ourselves. On reaching the small humpback bridge, we started to drive up, to go over, when the unexpected happened; just as we were driving up the small humpback bridge with the front windscreen of the car now sloping up at an angle, my son and I were able to see momentarily up into the clear blue sky without even trying. Upon looking up whilst still in our angled position within the car, I found myself looking at an unfamiliar object, stationary within the sky and silver in colour. The object was the size of a football in appearance; stopping the car at the required angle upon the bridge, I said to my son, upon sighting the object, 'What's that up there?'

My oldest son, who had also seen the strange object replied, 'I don't know.' Looking at this strange phenomenon within the clear blue sky, we could see that this motionless object was just sitting there, as if it were a part of the scenery. As we were looking up at the silver football, the silver object disappeared. It then reappeared momentarily in the same position. There was no cloud to cloak the object in any way. This silver object disappeared and reappeared upon its own axis three times for no apparent reason. Upon its third return to sight, it then, with tremendous speed, shot across the clear blue sky with a speed not normally known to man upon this earth. The speed was unmeasurable.

One and a half weeks later, I had gotten another of my sons a job with myself and the first son upon the very same building site. Again we were all driving down the same country road upon a hot and clear morning towards the same humpback bridge; but this time, after passing completely over the bridge four yards further on, I had looked up into the clear blue sky once again. Upon looking up, I again asked, 'What's that up there?'

Both my sons and I were now looking skywards in togetherness. What we were all now looking at was another UFO that again looked to be the size of a football. But this time, it was red in colour with a silver rim. The sun and the moon were again both up together; but this time they were both a little bit smaller in size, and looked a little higher in the sky from the earth and just as colossal. As I was looking up at the glowing object high in the sky, my oldest son said, 'There are two objects up there, one slightly behind the other.'

I replied, 'No there aren't!'

My youngest son then said, 'Yes there are Dad; we both have sunglasses on; that's why we can see another one just behind the other one.'

As we were talking, we could hear the distant sound of a helicopter. The helicopter seemed to be heading straight for the UFO; but in truth it was an optical illusion; the helicopter was miles below the UFO. As the helicopter headed (in appearance) towards the red football with a silver rim, the object within the sky disappeared upon its axis. When the helicopter had passed miles under the object and away, the red football-type object with a silver rim reappeared. The helicopter then turned, to head back into the same flight path as before, below the stationary object. The red object with a silver rim again disappeared from sight. The helicopter then circled around and around, but the red football-type object did not return into view. Within the same air space, below upon the ground, there was an army or navy aerodrome. My sons and I were convinced that the base below had known about the object that was stationed high above them. There was no foreseeable activity taking place upon the aerodrome in response to the phenomenon above them. It is known that a public airline pilot can report a sighting; but military pilots are not allowed to. I am convinced that the military air force stationed upon the ground were in direct communication with the object above. I am also convinced that the object within the sky could change its appearance by cloaking and blending in with the background to make itself disappear, just like a stick insect upon a tree. In this case, blue against a clear blue sky. We all know that the government covers up this sort of sighting, and that there are people who will say it was clearly something else. Perhaps not now, but in time, this story will be proven to be the truth, even by today's sceptics. But there is one thing for sure, I know what I had seen, it was not a weather balloon, a mirage, a trick of the light, or an ordinary aircraft.

Mr Patrick Moore from the programme *The Sky at Night* suggested to myself by letter that it was an aircraft that I had seen. I'm sorry to say Mr Moore, you were not there at the time when we saw this object; how can a person with your amount of knowledge on space and beyond tell me that it must have been an aircraft? I think that our knowledgeable Mr Moore is being kept in the dark as to what is really out there. There is not one person upon this earth who will ever convince myself or my family that we had not seen and witnessed an actual space craft, and myself and my sons, a UFO. I now take with me wherever I go a camera. even though I think a future sighting will never again come my way. Having my entire family and now myself witnessing UFOs, I must admit, would be very hard to explain. But it happened. In truth, we do not expect people to believe in our story; but at the end of the day we don't really care what others believe, for we know it to be the truth, and that's what really matters. We also now know that there are people out there just like us, who have witnessed the truth as we have. We can only say believe in the truth of what you have witnessed, and above all, believe in yourself. Only time can prove to the world that the truth is out there.

The Sinking Ship

Some years ago, when I was a young lad, I had always wanted to go on to the big ships. A life upon the open sea was the life for me. I have always been very envious of my old school friends who had in their early life succeeded in their goal to be able to go around the world, and at the same time able to save a wage, which they could accumulate on their every trip. The thought of this appealed to me very much. As the years moved on, I thought more and more about trying to join a ship somewhere; but I hadn't a clue how to go about it. Still a young lad of about twenty years of age, I decided to go for it. After making up my mind, I made my way down to the local dock area in Southampton. In the dock area of Southampton were lots of assorted shipping offices where one might find that one could join the type of ship that one desires. Upon my arrival to the Southampton dockside, I entered one of the big shipping offices that catered for the big liners, such as the Queen Mary. On entering the big shipping office, I spoke to one of the young boy assistants who was standing directly behind a very large counter. After talking to the young assistant for ten minutes or so, and explaining to him my most intimate thoughts, imprisoned within my mind over the years, I asked, 'What would now be the best way to go about my long-standing ambitious dream?'

I was then told by the boy assistant that I should look at the only option that was open to an unskilled person to enter into a sea-going position. He then told me to come back in a week's time, as there just might be a vacancy as a deck-hand upon one of their liners. After listening to his expert knowledge and most valued advice, I left the shipping office full of joy and anticipation.

That following week, I returned to that same office full of eagerness, and expecting to make a start as a deck-hand upon my arrival. After entering that same big shipping office, I made a bee-line towards the very large counter, situated to the far side of the ground floor building; at the counter, I again spoke to the very same assistant as the week before. On speaking to him for the second time, my joy and anticipation suddenly came down with a thud; the boy assistant told me, in short, to come back again in another week's time as there was nothing for me. I was very disillusioned, and felt very let down. I entered that office full of beans, and left with that empty feeling; I felt totally demoralised. That following week, I again returned to that same shipping office; the answer was the same as the week before. I attended that same big shipping office each week for two months, to no avail. It got to the stage whereupon I had only to show my face at the entrance door, to see him shaking his head.

Towards the end of each of those separate weeks that passed by, I felt even more demoralised. I reached that stage in time when I was not a happy person. I felt myself slowly giving up the fight to become a seaman upon one of those magnificent ocean liners. Never having been to sea before, I felt as if I were being fobbed off by the shipping office and their employees for reasons unknown to myself. After my eighth appearance at that office, I finally succumbed to defeat, and I stepped out of their office for the last time. Outside of that shipping office upon the pavement, I just stood there with my hands in my pockets, in a motionless bewildered state of mind. I was feeling really down and rejected by all and totally demoralised, whilst I stood there looking at the noisy heavy traffic, that was passing by in uncountable numbers. I then looked further about myself, skywards in the direction of the very large cold stone and grimy buildings, towering above the moving traffic. The cold-looking stone buildings filled the dock road with grandeur and splendour as they loomed above the dusty shadows of the passing clouds, amid the smog and exhaust fumes of the day. I stood miserably watching the heavy traffic as it tore up and down in both directions on the dusty and very grimy smoky road before me. After standing and looking at the traffic for a moment or two, I looked to the other shipping offices, situated upon the other side of the road; amongst all the billboards and shipping signs, my eyes widened as I noticed a very long sign that read: *South Coast Sand and Ballast Company Ltd*. I could just see the very long sign flickering back at myself, from between the passing container lorries, and the exhaust smoke upon the busy dock road, just like an old silent movie. I suddenly felt a slight smile appear upon my own miserable face, and the lost butterflies within my stomach returning in abundance. Once again, I felt within myself an uplifting urge to try again; knowing now, that I had nothing to lose, as there were many other shipping offices that I could try. Upon making my way cautiously through the heavy traffic whilst crossing that dusty road to reach the other side, I again heard a voice within my head saying, 'Well this could be it, go for it!'

Finally, having reached the other side of the road, I found myself standing outside the shipping office beneath the very long sign. The shipping office had a highly polished brass plate upon its very cold and grimy looking stone wall entrance. Taking a deep breath, I then entered the building through two very large dark stained oak doors, that must have stood approximately ten feet in height. Now being that much bolder, I once again approached a very long counter. At the counter, I could see a lot of activity going on between the public and employees of the company, upon what must have been one of their busiest days; it was just like being in Waterloo Station, there were people everywhere.

As I stood leaning upon the counter looking at a multitude of people moving in every direction, I heard a person's voice behind myself asking, 'Can I help you, sir?'

Looking immediately behind myself, back in the direction of the counter, I could plainly see that the voice belonged to yet another young assistant. Nervously I replied, 'Yes!' I then asked the young boy assistant if there were any openings for a deck-hand aboard any of their vessels. To my delight, the answer was an immediate, 'Yes! When can you start?' he asked with a smile.

'I can start straight away,' I replied, feeling the butterflies re-fluttering within my stomach.

I was told by the boy assistant that I had to catch a train to Portsmouth; upon my arrival, I was to proceed a little further to a docking point upon the coastline where I was to pick up with a vessel moored at the quayside. The boy assistant then said that the company would pay the rail fare, and that I was to take the train to Portsmouth upon that following day.

The next day was soon upon me and I was now on my way to Portsmouth. Sitting upon the train, I was filled with thoughts of joy; I could not wait to get there. I was a very happy person. After all those weeks of let-downs, I was finally going out to sea upon a big ship. I had thoughts of saving vast amounts of money from my wages, just as my old school chums had done in the past. It took approximately one hour to reach Portsmouth Station from Southampton, and yet it seemed much longer. After the train journey, and a small journey by bus, I finally reached my destination.

There at the quayside, sitting high within the water, was my first, and what was to later be known to myself, my last ship. The ship at that time was empty, and was getting ready to leave the quayside to collect its second load of ballast for that day from the depths of the sea bed, upon open waters. Whilst standing there at the quayside, my heart skipped a beat as I looked at the vessel before me with wide open eyes. The ship was an old ship; a rust bucket; but it was my ship. After walking proudly up the gang plank with bag in hand, I introduced myself to all on board. The crew whom I could see around me at that time consisted of two deck-hands, who in appearance seemed to be typical fighting seamen; they were both approximately five feet six in height, and quite stocky in build; they were both in their thirties; looking at them, one could see that they were without a doubt trouble! The ship's captain was a small man in his forties; he was very thin, and approximately five feet five in height; the captain appeared to be a quiet man, with not too much to say at any given time. The captain's mate was approximately six feet in height; he was also in appearance a very quiet person; but unlike the captain, he was also of stocky build. The ship's cook, who was not too far away, was also about six feet in height; he was a very thin looking person with a pointed face, and approximately fifty years of age; he was a very sad greasy looking chap, who could have done with a good bath. The ship's engineer was also a very thin six-foot person who was standing by his engine room door and wearing a grubby white pair of overalls. I had, upon first boarding the ship, sensed an atmosphere, seemingly directed at myself for reasons unknown; I was to find out later that my senses were correct, though it was never really clear why.

One hour later, we set sail for the great open sea. The ship that I was sailing upon was a very old tanker called the *Sand Snipe*. The ship was covered in red rust and obviously lacked much-needed paint to the whole of its structure; it was not quite what I had in mind; but rust or no rust, I was still a very happy person. The ship's outer colouring was supposedly painted black, but the red rust from the ship's plating had corroded on through into the paintwork; it was, in its true sense, a rust bucket. The paint throughout the ship's inside decking was of a rusted white; the wheelhouse was also painted white, with rust overrunning the paint; the rust almost hid from view what little paint there was left. All the ships that were owned by the company had the names of birds written upon their bows for identification, such as the *Sand Gull* and the *Sand Snipe* etc. The ship that I was upon had very deep open holds for the storing of its cargo. The decking around the ship was very narrow with flimsy looking hand rails which ran all around the outer edges of the ship to stop one from falling overboard. This type of vessel would sail out into the deep waters to an area just off the coastline, to where one could no longer see land; when the ship has reached its destination, suction pipes would be then used to load sand or ballast from the sea bed. Running all around the lower outside ship's plating was a single continuous line of white paint that was approximately four inches wide; this is called a ship's marker; when the ship's holds are being loaded, the tanker will slowly sink down into the sea, until the sea has levelled itself in alignment with the ship's marker; when the ships' holds were fully loaded, the tanker would sit very low in the water; it was really the wrong time of the year for any person to have joined a ship such as this, and then to enter into the deep water. I myself experienced the worst kind of weather aboard ship whilst under sail aboard the *Sand Snipe*. If the sea got a little rough when the tanker was underway with a full load, the wash of the raging sea running over the centre of the ship's decking sometimes gave the illusion that the midship would not reappear up to the surface; the sea water raging upon the submerging centre of the ship would then roll back into the sea just as the ship swelled back up, with the sea not quite able to enter into the storage holds. It was very frightening; it looked at times as if the ship would sink down into the swells of the raging sea, and never return back to the surface. One would also think that the ship would break its own back, carrying its heavy load in the downward plunge back into the sea as it rode the menacing waves. When the ship moved downwards into the swell of the sea, the stern, wheel-house and the forward bow were the only parts of the ship that could be seen out of the water in bad weather.

I was upon that ship for three days and two nights; it seemed like three years. When I first met the vessel upon the dockside in Portsmouth, the vessel had only just off-loaded its first load of ballast. The off-loading was done by a very large crane upon the quayside with the use of a very big grab. After the ship had been unloaded, the crew and I would then sail that ship to an appointed place shown within a square upon a grid map, into deep water to where we could retrieve a second shipment of ballast for the return trip back to Portsmouth. The ship made three deliveries to Portsmouth docks; two of those deliveries were after I had joined the ship. Upon my new adventures aboard the ship, the crew were giving me a hard time. The problems that I encountered with the crew upon the retrieval of my first load from the deep water, and upon the return trip to Portsmouth quayside, were nothing to what was to follow. I consider myself very lucky to be alive today, to tell the tale of what actually happened upon all three of my voyages aboard the *Sand Snipe*, and that of 'The Sinking Ship'.

My story really starts here, from the very moment that I first set foot upon the *Sand Snipe*, and then put out to sea upon my new adventures. For three days, and two nights, I did not eat aboard ship, for reasons to be later explained further into the story. The ship that I was now upon was underway. One mile out to sea, I found that the other two deck-hands were very hostile and rather off-hand towards me, in a way that I could not understand; the two deck-hands did their best to keep me apart from themselves, throughout the whole time that I was on board ship; they would not really have a lot to do with me; I felt like a loner, lost within the great walls of the ship, with nowhere to go. Whilst we were on the move to the pick-up point for the collection of ballast from the sea bed, I was given a chipping hammer; with the chipping hammer I was ordered to chip away the old flaking paint from the inside forward bow of the ship, to make ready for the red leading. Red lead paint was an undercoat of paint that was applied to the walls of the ship, before a final top coat of paint could be applied. The ship looked as if it hadn't seen a new coat of paint since the day it was built. As I chipped away at the old paint, the other two deck-hands were sat looking at me upon a heavy coil of anchoring rope wearing smiles upon their faces. The captain and his mate were also looking down at me, from inside the wheel-house that towered above myself. Somehow I felt as if I were being had. Every time I looked around to the other two deck-hands, my looks were received with smirks. The sea started to get a little rough as we moved further onwards; it was in its wake forcing the ship to sway. Dressed in black oilskins and a black south-western rain hat, the waves descending down upon me with blowing winds, I chipped away at the old paint in uncon-trollable weather; the captain and his mate were still in the wheel-house looking back down at me with smiles whilst I braved the stormy weather; they had no intention of giving the order for me to stop what I was doing. I could just see through the blinding spray of the sea that fell upon my face time after time, that the other two deck-hands standing safe and dry within a sheltered part of the ship were both smirking as usual as they stood watching my every move. Looking at them, I had the feeling that it was some sort of challenge; Whatever it was, I was not going to give in. I had become very stubborn and obstinate in the course of my duties, and I decided there and then, to stay with it all the way; no matter what the fury of the sea might throw upon myself.

The closing of the day was almost upon us, and there was very little daylight left. The empty ship bounced about the waves like an empty corked bottle as it sat very high out of the water; I held on for dear life with one hand on the safety railing as I chipped away at the old paint with the other upon the inside forward bow; I was now awash with the wind and spray of the sea. As the sea smashed violently against the sides of the ship, I got quite wet, even though my body was covered in oilskins from head to foot; I felt very seasick; but I still would not give in, no matter what the sea had continued to throw at me. The journey to the pick-up point had taken four hours, we finally reached our destination just as the sea and the winds became much calmer. Whatever it was that they all hoped to see, did not happen, for their smiles had faded with the winds. On arrival at our destination, all anchors were set loose and everything set into motion. The sky was now quite dark, and the ship was ablaze with lights, which illuminated the surrounding waters; I could see the ship's reflection as I gazed back down into the water. The anchors were not just for holding the ship fast to the sea bed, they were also used to co-ordinate an alignment by having an anchor attached to the winches upon all four corners of the ship. The winches were set front and rear of the ship to give a criss-cross pattern to enable the ship to suck up the ballast through the suction pipes to fill the ship's holds. Whilst the captain and his mate were manipulating the ship in coordination and alignment with the winches for the sucking up of ballast, I was able to leave my post to go and find the cookhouse, as I was now very hungry; I had been aboard the ship for some twelve hours or more, and it was now time for myself to fill my own empty holds.

Upon finding the cookhouse, I was very surprised by how tiny it was; the cookhouse was full of steam from the very large iron pots upon the stoves; the lack of ventilation caused the steam to run back down the steel plated discoloured cream walls that hadn't seen a scrubbing brush in years. On looking around the cookhouse, I could see that it was no bigger than approximately six foot by eight foot. The cooking stoves themselves, were very big; there was not very much room for the cook to operate with sufficient ease whilst preparing the meals; the heat from the cooking stoves was immense; there was also a great lack of air within the cookhouse. Adjoining the cookhouse was a very small dining-room with no actual door between the two; the heat coming out from the cookhouse into the dining area was very intensive and overpowering. On looking around the small dining area that measured approximately the same as the cookhouse, I could not miss the other two deck-hands who had reached the cookhouse before me; they were both grinning like a pair of Cheshire cats whilst sitting and waiting for their meals beside a small dining-table. The table was covered by an off-white stained table-cloth. Upon the table-cloth were two salt and pepper containers, and a sauce bottle without its top; the neck of the sauce bottle was covered with an overspill of stale dried sauce. By the look of the dining-room and the kitchen's steel plated walls; they too could have done with a new coat of paint. There were four chairs around the table, including the two occupied by the other two deck-hands. As I sat down opposite the other two deck-hands, in stepped the cook from the cookhouse. What was to follow, I will never forget for the rest of my life.

When the ship's cook stepped into the dining area towards the table, I could see upon his forehead a headband absolutely saturated with running sweat. I have never ever seen a person sweat like it in the whole of my life, it was cascading everywhere; it was just as if someone had placed a hose-pipe up the back of his very badly stained T-shirt, with the end of the hose concealed to the back of his head to give the illusion of a built-in waterfall, escalating back down from his forehead. I was then overcome by horror and disbelief as I watched him fill three drinking mugs from a very large metal teapot. No sooner had he tipped about an egg-cup-full of tea into each drinking mug, with one sweeping movement of the teapot across the mugs; the sweat from his head came as a downfall of rain filling the rest of the drinking mugs to overflowing. I felt sick; it was totally unbelievable. The off-white table-cloth was now even more stained as the sweat had fallen on to the table from the overspill. The overspill continued on down to the floor to where the cook was standing; in its wake, the tea-tinted sweat formed a very large puddle about his feet. I was then amazed to see the other two deck-hands pick up a mug each, then drink the slops from the mugs as if it were quite normal and acceptable to everyday life. The ship's cook, who was in bad need of a wash and shave, returned to his cookhouse just as the two other deck-hands started to chat to each other. As I sat there, I looked casually down to the wet footprints now trailing behind the cook as he entered his smoky cave. Feeling sick, I pointed out to the other two crew members what I had just seen, and what they were both now drinking. They both looked back at me for a moment, then started to laugh.

One of the two deck-hands replied, 'It's good for you! Get it down ya!'

I just sat there in overwhelming disbelief at their total

acceptance of the reality of it all. I then looked down at the badly stained drinking mug before me as I rested my elbows on the off-white stained table-cloth, with my chin resting in the cups of my hands. I thought, Now I've seen it all. But there was worse to come. Within the next moment, the ship's cook reappeared from the cookhouse. Along his right arm, he held two deep dinner plates; across the same shoulder hung a grubby and very stained tea-towel; in his left hand, he was holding another dinner plate. The plates had within them what appeared to be a roast dinner gone wrong. As the cook placed the plates on the table in front of himself, just for a moment in time, one could see what looked like a very shallow amount of gravy, within the inside bottom base of the dinner plates; in that same moment of time, whilst he stood momentarily over the plates, before he had time to push them at speed away from himself in the direction of each crew member, down came this torrent of sweat, filling each plate in turn to overflowing, just as he had done with the drinking mugs; the colour of the gravy turned a transparent light brown from a deep brown.

As I sat there, I watched the almost transparent gravy overflow the lip edge of the dinner plates, and then run back on to the table-cloth; it was as if I were in a living dream, a nightmare come to life. The ship's cook returned to his cookhouse moments after he had pushed the dinners towards each crew member, but not before mopping his over-wet headband, and a part of his forehead along with the back of his neck with the badly stained tea-towel, that had previously hung heavily upon his right shoulder. I then looked to the other two deck-hands as they both picked up a dessert spoon each; one of them started to laugh as the other deck-hand ravishingly got stuck into the slop meal. I just sat there looking at them with my arms now folded upon the table; to think that I had only been aboard for twelve hours or so, with two more nights and three days to go.

As I looked over at them both, one of the deck-hands looked up in my direction, just as he was about to shovel down his slop dinner with a very large dessert spoon, and said as before, 'Get it down ya! It's good for ya!'

They both made me feel quite ill as I sat there with my elbows once again resting upon the table, and with both hands covering my eyes. I had thoughts on how could I possibly get through this ordeal for another three days without food, as there was no way that I was going to eat that slop. No sooner had the deck-hand spoken, than I looked down at the swamp before me from between the gaps of my fingers, just as the palms of my hands covered the remainder of my face; I decided enough was enough. Standing upon my feet, I very quickly left the dining area just as the other two once again started to shovel down their swamp meal with the large dessert spoons.

As time slowly passed, I found myself absolutely starving and drained of all strength; but as luck would have it, I had in my bag a small bar of chocolate; this small bar of chocolate had somehow so see me through my hunger and journey's end.

Chocolate and fresh water rationed to myself, was all that I consumed whilst serving upon that prison ship for two nights and three days. I lost quite a bit of body weight during my time aboard the *Sand Snipe*. I had no intention of returning to the cookhouse, I would rather starve.

Early morning was now upon us, and we were back on course to Portsmouth docks to off-load my first shipment of ballast. Finally we made port, but there were no shops at hand for me to replenish my own private stock of food. It looked as if I would have to go upon a crash diet for the remainder of my time aboard ship. After the unloading, we again set sail for yet another load to be delivered back to the same port. On sailing back out into deep water, I kept very clear of the cookhouse whilst enduring menacing remarks from the two other deck-hands. It was now quite late, darkness fell about us. The night was long and I was feeling very tired; I was able to grab a little sleep within the crews' cabin whilst the ship was being loaded.

The following morning, we were loaded and on our way back to Portsmouth with the second load, and I was feeling very weak through the lack of food; I started to think about the other two deck-hands; there were times I could have set about the pair of them, but I would not lower myself, even though I had the capabilities to do so.

Upon reaching Portsmouth, the off-loading began. As time passed, and the off-loading was nearing its end, everyone was getting ready to move the ship back out and away from the quayside. The ship's motors once again started up; we were now on our way out and heading in the direction of the open sea. We were now going to pick up one more load of ballast that was bound for the Southampton docks. When loaded, the delivery was to be taken to a place called Dibles Wharf, this being a part of the Southampton docks; Dibles Wharf was not too far from the gasworks area of Northam, this also being my home town and my salvation. We finally reached the re-dredging point by mid-morning.

Once again, the heavy anchoring chains thundered on down into the sea; the ship was very soon loading its precious cargo. Having some free time on my hands, I sat down upon the ship's deck for a relaxing cigarette whilst the other two deck-hands passed quite near to me, then started to get a little pushy for no real reason; I warned them both to lay off me, but they just looked at me then laughed.

I then said to them, 'Look! I can handle myself if I have the need to; I've a few judo belts to back it up.'

They again both laughed; but I did notice that as they did so, they moved a little further away from myself.

We finished loading early that afternoon. It was now up anchors and on course for the Southampton docks. To save future trouble whilst aboard the ship, I reported the incident to the captain and his mate within the control room. On seeing the captain and his mate, I explained what happened in regard to the other two deck-hands, and cook within the cookhouse. The captain and his mate just stood staring to the front of themselves, whilst steering the ship upon its navigational course. As they both stood looking out of the control room window they turned their heads for a fleeting moment in my direction, then back to the window. One could not hear a pin drop in the stillness of an unnatural deathly silence. It was as if I were invisible and upon a ghost ship, for they had not said a word in reply. It was again as if time itself had stood still. After standing there for a moment or two and looking at them, I again repeated what I had said; again they both turned their heads in my direction; but this time, they both gave me a smirk just as the cook appeared with a mug of sweat-filled tea for them both to drink. As I stood there looking at them, I thought to myself, this smirking must be some sort of ship's disease. The reading that I got from their facial expressions was that I would have to face any other problems that might occur on my own, whilst I was stuck on board ship.

After looking at them both for a moment or two, I turned to face the exit door of the control room, and I left the control room in disgust and total disbelief; their interest in the crews' welfare was nil. I could now only think about the journey's end, the sooner that I could get off this ship the better.

Time slowly passed as I stood upon the ship's decking watching the heavily loaded ship push on through the water, with the wash of the sea foaming up against the sides of the ship's forward bow. It was now late afternoon, and I was happy to see land ahead; I could clearly see the South-ampton docks. I was once again, a very happy person. Upon the ship's approach into Southampton docks, the daylight began to fade. The ship finally came to a stop within the Southampton water lane alongside two old timber barges, anchored upon floating buoys. The order was given to drop the anchor quite near to the old barges. I could scarcely believe it; we were only a short distance from the docking area, from where we were now anchored; one could see dry land approximately eight hundred yards from either side of the midship. I then asked one of the deck-hands if we are going ashore by lowering a lifeboat into the sea from the side of the ship; both deck-hands laughed as one of them replied, 'No! We are here for the night.'

I was quite taken aback by what they said in reply.

One of the deck-hands then said, pointing a finger in the direction of the docks, 'We will off-load over there in the morning; as it is, there's no one there at this time of night, and their gates to the road will be locked, so we're stuck here for the night; there will not be anyone over there until early morning,' he added with a smirk.

The two deck-hands then walked a little further along the ship's deck away from myself. I was now feeling very upset, hungry, and very tired. Whilst leaning upon the safety railings, I looked down into the dockland's murky water as it moved with its own currents. It was now quite dark; a full moon was on the way up. Looking out and across to what was now a well-lit docking bay at the quayside, I felt, as usual, very low and miserable as another hour dragged slowly by; it seemed as if the night were never going to end. I then looked back down into the dark murky waters of the flowing tide, and wished a passing row boat would happen by, but I knew that it could only be in my dreams. I then looked back along the decking to where the other two deck-hands were sat looking back at me; both were whispering and smirking and giggling like two year olds. On looking at them, I knew that I had only to put up with them till morning and then I would be home free.

The next three hours slipped by quite quickly; the moon was now nearly at its fullest. I was once again situated with my arms folded upon the railings looking out and across the waters at the reflecting moonlight that illuminated the white foamy wash, that was now striking up against the base of the docking bay. The ship was now moving slightly upon its moorings with the flowing current of the tide. Looking back down into the black murky water below, I could see driftwood and all sorts of rubbish passing by. As I looked upon the floating rubbish, I thought to myself, What a dirty old world this is.

Whilst I was momentarily in thought, something very big and heavy hit the lower ship's plating with a thud; leaning over and out from the safety railings to get a better view of what it was that had hit the outer lower side of the ship with such force, I could see that it was a half-submerged heavily waterlogged railway sleeper. At some point in time, the old railway sleeper must have fallen into the sea from the dockside. Stepping up upon the safety railings to get a better view of the passing railway sleeper, I stretched out and over a little further, to watch the heavy lump slide aside the ship with the tide. As it passed on, it was then that I noticed something was not quite right; if it was not for the driftwood hitting the side of the ship with such force, I would not have noticed that the ship was in mortal danger of sinking. Upon looking down to where the passing sleeper had struck the ship, I could not believe my eyes. I could no longer see the ship's water-level markings aside the ship, even though the night was very bright from the full moon. Jumping back down very quickly from the safety railings, I immediately moved very fast along the ship's deck towards the other two deck-hands, who were sat upon a pile of spare anchoring rope nearby.

On finally reaching them, I shouted, 'The ship is sinking! The ship is sinking!'

The two deck-hands fell about laughing.

I repeated angrily, 'I tell you! The ship is sinking!'

The more I tried to warn them, the more they both fell about laughing. I then gave them a pitiful look, as I watched them both roll about the ship's deck in fits of laughter. As I stood there watching them laughing at me with tears in their eyes, a thought came to mind; there I was, a seaman of three days, telling them who had been at sea for the best part of their lives, that the ship was about to sink.

'Go tell the old man!' one of them said hysterically whilst still rolling about the ship's deck with laughter.

Knowing that he meant the ship's captain, I looked at them both in silence for a moment, then walked back to the same part of the safety railings that I had previously occupied. Looking back down into the running tide to the reflection of the moon that was casting an array of golden lights across the surface of the water, I then began to look for other answers to what I had seen, in regards to the disappearance of the ship's marker. Now with my head as empty as my stomach, I had thoughts as to whether they were right or not. It could be my imagination; or maybe it was the bright moonlight giving me an optical illusion, thus making it look like the ship's level marking was not really there. Perhaps it was a trick of the light? After all, when one strains one's eyes into the darkness of the night long enough, things do not always appear to be what they really are; shadows move if one stares long enough at a fixed single point; or was it that I'd gone a little mad? Maybe that was it! Gone a little mad with the effects from what has been happening aboard this ship. After all was said and done, I had seen things aboard this ship that take some believing; I suppose it's quite possible that one's imagination can run wild through hunger. As I was deep in thought looking for answers, and doubting my own sanity, I again looked over the side of the ship to see if the ship's water-level marking was truly there; focusing my eyes on the lower part of the ship's plating, I could see that it was definitely not there. I then fixed my eyes upon a paint scratch that was aside the lower part of the outside ship's plating; this then gave myself a new substitute water-level marking that was situated just above the present sea level, where the sea was menacingly lapping at the ship's side. To take the strain away from my eyes a little, and to clear my mind, I looked up and out across the river to the well-lit docking bay opposite; I then glanced up at the very large cranes that stood towering in the bright moonlight. The sky behind the large cranes was full of stars, it was a magnificent sight. The night emitted a fresh breeze along with the stench of the sea; I had thoughts of fishing to pass the time, and possibly at the same time, to fill my empty stomach with the catch.

Another hour slowly passed as I looked back down into the murky water below, then again to the lower ship's plating; upon looking to the ship's outside plating, I could not see where my new substitute ship's level marker was situated. Climbing back up upon the safety railings, and then again stretching out and over for a better view, I then looked back down to where I had last seen the paint scratch aside the ship; there was no sign of my new marker. I then searched in the depths with straining eyes, down deeper into the shadowy deep water upon the lower side of the ship, then beyond the water level. After a moment or two I found it; I then momentarily froze upon the railings as I saw that the paint scratch was now well below the sea level. I could barely see my new water-level mark through the murky sea water, that was still menacingly lapping at the sides of the ship. Now I knew that I was right, the ship was without a doubt sinking. Jumping back down from the railings once again, I raced along the ship's deck to find the other two deck-hands. On finding them further along the ship, I again told them that the ship was sinking; again they went straight into fits of laughter.

I then shouted above their laughter, 'Believe it or not! I'm telling you! The ship really is going to sink!'

The sound of my voice fell upon deaf ears, and I felt like the little boy who cried wolf. With uncontrollable laughter, they once again told me to go and see the old man. With tears in their eyes, they both simultaneously pointed to the captain's cabin door nearby. I then looked to the door that they were pointing to, then back at them.

'We dare you to go and wake him up, and tell him what you keep telling us,' one of them said as they both roared with laughter.

I looked at the two hyenas and replied, 'I will!'

It was now twelve o'clock midnight. On reaching the captain's cabin door, I grabbed at the shadowy handle upon the cold steel surface plating; throwing open the iron door with a loud bang to the amazement of the two deck-hands, I stepped into the captain's cabin; the captain was fast asleep with his back to me laid upon the top bunk-bed with a single blanket for a covering. The captain's mate was also asleep within the lower bunk; neither of them had moved upon the sound of the door being thrown open with such a loud bang.

I then shouted, 'Hoy! Wake up! We're sinking!'

The captain turned very slowly upon his side under the blanket until he was facing me. The captain's mate was undisturbed and appeared to be fast asleep upon his stomach. The bright moonlight was now shining into the small room through the open door from behind my own person, and cast a shadow of myself across the bunk-beds.

238

The captain then turned his back to me once again by slowly turning under his blanket to face the wall.

I again shouted to his silhouette upon the bunk-bed to the far side of the room, 'Wake up! Wake up! We're sinking!'

The captain, without moving, replied in a soft voice, 'Yes, all right, shut the door on your way out.'

I then repeated my outburst even louder. 'But we're sinking! I'm telling you! Sinking!'

'Yeah! Yeah, all right, shut the door behind you,' replied the captain once again with an unconcerned soft voice. The captain then pulled the blanket over his head to block out the sound of my voice, and the light from the moon that beamed on through into his cabin from the open doorway.

I just stood there for a moment looking at the two motionless shadowy shapes upon the bunk-beds. On shaking my head with further disbelief, I turned to face the entrance door; I then muttered to myself, 'I don't believe it. We're sinking! And he wants to sleep.'

On leaving the captain's cabin, I slammed shut the cabin door; the outside steel wall structure of his cabin shook with the force of the door slamming tight behind myself. The two hyenas were just outside still laughing. As I passed the two deck-hands, I could see the ship's cook throwing his sweaty meal slops over the side of the ship, just as he gave me a guilty sorrowful look. What he had thrown over board was most probably what he had put aside for me throughout the day. I then made my way back along the ship's deck to the very same location as before. I decided there and then that there was no way on this earth that I was going to sleep that night. No longer feeling hungry, I forced myself to stay awake all that night.

Morning was once again upon us. We had all somehow survived the night. It was now six in the morning, I was very tired and stiff from the night air. Everyone on board was now up and about. The ship's cook brought a mug of slop tea for me to drink; he must have been silently watching my every move from the start of my voyage. Placing the grubby mug in my hand, he looked at me sympathetically before slowly turning to walk away. Still with my arms partially folded upon the safety railing with mug in hand, I tossed the slop tea into the sea; the empty heavily stained mug followed the slop into the sea with a splash, as the mug hit the water. Looking down into the water, I watched the mug drift slightly with the current before disappearing with a gurgle of bubbles to the bottom of the sea. As I stood there, I heard the clanking of heavy anchor chains being pulled up. It was a gladdening sound to my ears. The ship's engines had started up, and we were on the move. I turned from the railings only to see the other two deck-hands coiling up three very large and heavy ship's hawser ropes, that had been used as an extra mooring rope by tying the ship to the old barges. They both now looked almost sorry for me. The front of the ship had now swung around to face the docking area. Slowly we crossed the narrow river in the direction of the quayside. We were now approximately six hundred yards from the anchorage of the docking bay. My heart once again skipped a beat as we moved nearer to that place of safety. The ship was almost at a stop as we neared the docking bay nose on. It was all engines stop. We were drifting inward, still nose on. We were now approximately fifty yards from the docking area. Then something happened. The ship came to a sudden stop with a jolt upon the high tide at approximately ten yards from the docking bay for no apparent reason. The engines started up again for manoeuvring. Using the ship's engines, the captain edged the ship forward with nudging movements. But the ship still refused to move further in. Several attempts were made to get the ship moving forward, by using the ship's engines; but it was of no use. The ship stopped at approximately the same ten yards from the docking bay as before. It was very clear to myself, that this ship was going nowhere. It was now all engines stop. The captain and his mate came down from the wheel-house to see just what was holding us back. There they all stood; the captain and his mate, the other two deck-hands, the ship's cook, and the ship's engineer, who had only appeared from his engine room for the second time since the start of my voyage. The captain was now standing to the front of the ship's bow scratching his head with his fingers. The captain's mate was standing aside the captain with his hands upon his hips, shaking his head in disbelief. The engineer was now standing next to them wiping his hands into an oily rag. The ship's cook was standing nearby still wearing the same badly stained T-shirt and headband. The other two deck-hands, minus their smirks, were now looking over the front of the bow together, to see what was in the water holding us back.

I then suddenly caught the ship's smirking disease, as I heard the captain say to his mate, 'There must be a mud bank down there.'

'I don't think so,' replied the mate, 'it was quite clear last week.'

I then moved a little closer to the captain and his mate, interrupting the two by saying, 'I told you! We're sinking; but none of you will listen.'

The captain just looked at me with a half smile, then turned to the mate and remarked, 'It's got to be a mud bank holding us back! It can't be anything else.'

The mate said nothing, he just shook his head in half agreement. The captain then gave the order to have a rope thrown from the front of the ship to a bollard that was situated upon the docking bay. Upon the docking bay there was also a yard worker who had not long clocked on for work. The yard worker was just standing and watching our every move, he must have sensed that we had a problem on board. On seeing a deck-hand throwing across a line, the yard worker immediately grabbed for it as it fell in his direction. The line, this being a very thin twine with a weight upon the throwing end, was attached to a very thick heavy anchoring rope, that was laid coiled upon the ship's deck; after catching the thin line, the yard man pulled it towards himself, until he was able to take a hold of the heavy anchoring rope attached to the other end of the throwing line. The yard man then placed the loop end of the anchoring rope over a nearby bollard that is used to anchor ships to the quayside. The captain was now back within his wheel-house. The engineer was also now back in the engine room. At the bow of the ship, the captain's mate stayed to keep a watchful eye on what was happening. With the use of the spare anchoring rope and the ship's engines, the captain and his mate started once again to try and move the ship forward. The winch pulling upon the rope was under great strain; the ship's engines were trying to ease the strain upon the winch. After all their efforts, the ship still refused to move. Suddenly the spare anchoring rope snapped under the great strain of the winch and the ship's engines. It was all stop! The captain's mate then ordered a wire rope to be thrown across to the yard worker in preference to another ordinary anchoring rope, by the same method as before. But this time two wire ropes and both forward winches were used along with the ship's engines, to ensure a better chance of the ship getting into port. When everything was in readiness, the mate signalled the captain; together, the two winches and the ship's engines again tried to move the ship forward. At last the ship was slowly moving forward under an enormous strain upon both winches of the ship's engines. As time slowly passed, they were finally able to manoeuvre the ship into its docking position alongside the docking bay. When everything had been tied down and made secure, the ship's engines were turned off, and I was now ready to call it a day. I had now only to see the captain to tell him that I was leaving the ship for good and this docking bay was my last stop. After leaving the ship's deck, I made my way up to the wheel-house. On entering the wheel-house, I once again confronted the captain and his mate. I told the captain that I was leaving the ship and that I would not be back. The captain and his mate just looked at me, then gave that same old ship's disease smirk as before. I stood there looking back at them both; a moment or two passed by in total silence.

I then said, 'Smirk as much as you like, it's not going to make any difference to your present situation; I'm still telling you, the ship is sinking!'

They both smirked even more as I turned to leave the wheel-house. After leaving the wheel-house, I made my way back down to the ship's lower deck. On reaching the lower deck with my bag in hand, I walked towards the gang plank that ran up from the ship to the quayside; my gateway to freedom. As I started to walk off the ship by means of the gang plank, the other two deck-hands gave me a whistling sound; it was the same sound that is given to the captain when he leaves the ship. I then stopped upon the gang plank; I looked back down at the two deck-hands, who were situated upon the ship's deck below and laughing. On looking back down to them, I said spitefully, 'You have had your laughs, just think about what I am saying to you both, the time will come when I will have the last laugh; I hope you all go down with the ship. Sometime in the very near future, both you and the crew will find that I was right about this ship sinking; enjoy your slop dinners, it might be your last.'

After I stopped talking to them, I gave them the ship's smirk, then moved on up the gang plank towards the docking bay. The big cranes had started to off-load the ship as I was about to leave the yard; on leaving the yard, I made my way back to the big shipping offices in Canute Road, Southampton. At the shipping office, I told them to make up my money and cards as my dream was now over. I also told them about all that had happened upon that ship, and that their ship was going to sink. At first, they too smiled the famous smirk, then their smiles disappeared as they realised that I was quite serious and in deadly earnest as to what I was saying.

One week after my ordeal upon that ship, I regained my lost weight and was glad to be home. I decided to go and look for work that following week. Leaving my home about mid-morning, I drove my car from Southampton to Hythe. In Hythe there was a firm called Husband's Ship Yard that repaired all large sea-going vessels. Upon walking into their yard, and about to pass the slipway, I stopped to ask a yard worker for directions to the personnel office. As he was giving me the directions, I noticed a very large ship up on their slipway, where they repaired all the ships. The ship was sitting high out of the water upon several very large wooden blocks. Each huge wooden block was as big as a steam roller. I asked the yard worker, after he had given me the directions for the personnel office, 'What's the name of that ship up there hanging out to dry? It looks very familiar.'

'It's the *Sand Snipe*,' the yard worker replied obligingly.

'Why is it there? I only sailed upon that last week.'

The yard worker replied, 'The whole of the bottom is full of holes and rust, it's as rotten as a pear.'

I then looked to the underside of the ship from a distance. As I stood beside the yard man, I could see quite a few holes upon the red rust-covered underside, that left me lost for words.

I then remarked, 'That ship should have sunk whilst we

were at sea, I have never seen anything like it.'

The yard worker stood shaking his head in agreement as he then said, 'The shipping companies do not really know what to do with the ship, their insurers cannot make up their minds whether to renew the whole of the bottom half of the ship, or to scrap the whole thing.'

After listening to what the yard worker was saying, I walked closer to where the ship was situated upon the very large wooden blocks, with the yard worker following close behind. Looking up the bottom of the ship from underneath, I could see holes in the bottom, that looked as if the whole underside had been sprayed by machine-gun bullets; the holes were about half an inch in circumference. I will never know just how that ship stayed afloat. The whole underside was also completely covered in red running rust. Looking at the amount of holes that peppered the underside platings, it would be right to assume that the ship must have held thousands of gallons of sea water within its bulk heads right throughout the hull; with the combined weight of the ship's cargo, the sea water, and the ship's own weight, the ship must have been dragging upon the sea bed, creating its own mud bank as it strained to get itself into the docking area; this in turn caused the pulling rope that was attached to the winch to snap. I then stepped back from under the ship in amazement at what I had just seen, with the thought of how lucky I was to have been able to have survived a sinking that was without a doubt going to happen if the ship had stayed in the water; a sinking that should have taken place during my time aboard her; it was a frightening thought.

Turning to the yard worker, I said, 'I told them all when I was on board that ship, that it was sinking; they wouldn't believe me, they just kept laughing; I would like to have been a fly upon their office wall when they all finally realised that I was right about their ship sinking.' With a smile, I looked to the yard worker, emphasising, 'Now it's my turn to smirk and laugh.'

Looking back at the whole incident, I am now very sure and confident that the crew aboard that ship will never forget me to the end of their days. I told them all upon leaving the ship at the quayside that I would have the last laugh, and that's exactly what I am doing; having the last laugh. As for that new job that I had gone to Husband's Ship Yard for, I didn't get it.